"This study may be the most important 50 days of your life! Whether you are new in Christ or a veteran Christ-Follower, seeing God with 20/20 vision will re-energize your faith, recalibrate your perspective, and transform your relationships. I highly recommend it."

CHIP INGRAM, Teaching Pastor, Living on the Edge; author of *Holy Ambition, God as He Longs for You to See Him*, and more

"With winsome and engaging writing, René Schlaepfer paints an extraordinary depiction of our God. And along the way he quietly reminds us that this is the God in whose image we are made. So this devotional sneaks up on you—it doesn't just reintroduce you to God, but also to yourself."

M. CRAIG BARNES, senior pastor, Shadyside Presbyterian Church, author of *Sacred Thirst, Hustling God*, and more

"Ever feel like, when it comes to your faith, you've heard it all before? I come from a lifetime of ministry, yet I found sparkling, fresh new stories and insights in René Schlaepfer's newest book, *God Is*. It inspired and motivated me. And I know this book will refresh and enrich your spiritual life too. You'll laugh, you'll learn, you'll be glad you read it!"

BILL BUTTERWORTH, speaker and author, *On The Fly Guide to Balancing Work, Life*; *When Life Doesn't Turn Out Like You Planned*, and more

"The heartbeat of this book is a genuine passion for God! As René suggests, read *God Is* in tandem with the Bible and watch your heart expand as you gaze on the beauty of the Maker of all things... I am confident you will meet God in fresh and powerful new ways. Have fun!"

REV. DR. KEVIN G. HARNEY, Lead Pastor of Shoreline Community Church and author of *Seismic Shifts*, *The U-Turn Church*, and *Organic Outreach for Churches*

GOD IS

A 50-Day Exploration of God's Attributes

BY RENÉ SCHLAEPFER

"GOD IS: A 50-day exploration of God's attributes"
© 2011 Twin Lakes Church, Inc.
ISBN 978-1-4507-9144-1

If you would like to reproduce or distribute any part of this publication, please contact us:
Twin Lakes Church, 2701 Cabrillo College Drive, Aptos, CA 95003-3103, USA
or email info@tlc.org

CONTENTS

DAY 0
INTRODUCTION

GOD IS....

How do you finish that sentence?

God is remote.

    God is unfair.

        God is uncaring.

            God is irrelevant.

                God is indulgent.

                    God is absurd.

                        God is unknowable.

                          God is me.

                            God is dead.

A.W. Tozer said, "What we believe about God is the most important thing about us." [1]

It's true.

1

What you believe about God can make you

    courageous or fearful

      joyful or sad

        spiritually energized or drained.

Yet most of us spend very little time really examining what we believe about God.

In fact, we humans often picture God as just a super-sized version of things here on earth. You might think it's easy to spot this tendency in the handmade idols of ancient peoples because much of their god-imagery looks to us like giant warriors, or giant animals. Those idols obviously reflect their own time, their own fears, their own fashions. But are we any different?

I'll admit it. At various times in my life I have imagined God as one of these modern idols:

God is a Galactic Grandpa. Worthy of respect, but not really relevant for today.

God is a Cosmic Cop. Aiming His sin radar gun at me just when I'm having fun. Waiting to bust me.

God is a Supernatural Slot Machine. I put in my prayers, pull the lever, and the results… well, they're unpredictable. Sometimes I hit the jackpot. Mostly I'm disappointed. But I'll keep trying, because you just never know.

God is a Frightening Father. You might see God as unpredictable, showing flashes of anger followed by torrents of generosity. So you're always on guard. Uncertain. Untrusting.

God is a Big Blur. Like a massive abstract painting with an obscure meaning. He's the Force, or a Feeling, or the First Cause. But He's not personal. And He sure doesn't care about me.

But I've found that the real God is far bigger, and far wilder, and far more exciting and powerful and comforting, than any of my preconceptions.

HOW DO I THINK ABOUT GOD?

One of the most popular series PBS television ever did was called *Searching for God in America.* The producers interviewed people from all walks of life and put together a fascinating pastiche of religion in this country as they asked them one simple question: "What is God like?"

That's precisely the question I'm asking in this book.

Only I'm not taking public opinion polls, as valuable as they can be as a barometer of religious trends. That's because mere human opinion doesn't get me much higher than human imagination. And thoughts about the actual God must by definition stagger the imagination.

So in this book I'll be looking at a source that challenges and inspires me far beyond than my own preconceived ideas: The Bible.

It's the best-selling book of all time. It's the inspired Word of God. Yet it's not very well known to most people today. Often it's not really *read* as much as *read into,* used as a gimmick to prove whatever notions people bring to it. But I think you'll find that what the Bible *really* teaches about *God* is very different than the caricature many people have of Christian theology.

A MIND OPEN TO GOD

If you're thinking, *"been there, done that"* let me encourage you to keep an open mind.

Are you open to the possibility, however slight you may imagine it to be, that you haven't learned all there is to learn about God? That maybe — just maybe — some of the preconceived notions you have about the traditional biblical view of God are challenged by the Bible itself?

Then read on.

ENJOYING THE GREATEST MYSTERY

This book is like unraveling a great mystery, the greatest mystery of all time: *Who is God?*

It's a puzzle no human can ever fully solve of course, but every day you'll discover another piece to add to the puzzle, see a new dot to connect to the other dots, so that you'll slowly begin to discern an outline of the Beauty behind all other beauties, the Power behind all powers.

We're not the first investigators. Each day in this study you and I will consider what ancient God-detectives, the theologians of the past, called *attributes of God* — truths about God's nature and being. They are puzzle pieces: Pithy, powerful, poetic ways to describe the divine. And they are awesome. Mind-blowing.

4

And these clues are being left for us by God Himself. *He wants to be caught.*

WHAT I WAS MADE FOR

What you discover about God will secure some of your secret hopes, surpass some of your wildest imaginings, and spin some of your own concepts sideways.

And you'll find something else: *The reason you exist.*

When you discover more about God, you'll feel something inside stirring, a resonance you may not have felt in a long while.

That's what it feels like to be doing what you were made for.

As J.R.R. Tolkien, author of *The Lord of the Rings*, said:

> The chief purpose of life, for any one of us, is to increase according to our capacity our knowledge of God by all means we have, and to be moved by it to praise and thanks. To do, as we say in *Gloria in Excelsis*: "We praise you, we call you holy, we worship you, we proclaim your glory, we thank you for the greatness of your splendor." [2]

So enjoy this journey further into the greatness of His splendor! You'll be surprised and challenged and enlightened each day as you dare to finish this sentence:

God is...

GOD IS

Self-revelatory
Holy
Beautiful

One of the most wonderful things about knowing God is that there's always so much more to know, so much more to discover. Just when we least expect it, He intrudes into our neat and tidy notions about who He is and how He works. JONI EARECKSON TADA

DAY 1
GOD THIRST

READ YOUR BIBLE: *Psalm 63:1–5*

SPOTLIGHT VERSE: *God, you are my God. I search for you. I thirst for you like someone in a dry, empty land where there is no water.* PSALM 63:1 (NCV)

WE THIRST FOR GOD. Across time, across cultures:

ISRAEL, 1000 B.C.

The Hebrew King David sings, *"As the deer pants for streams of water, so my soul pants for you, my God. My soul thirsts for God, for the living God."* (PSALM 42:1–2A)

NORTH AFRICA, 400 A.D.

The Roman author Augustine writes: "God, you have made us for yourself, and our hearts are restless till they find their rest in you." [3]

PARIS, FRANCE, 1600 A.D.

French mathematician Blaise Pascal observes: "There is a God-shaped vacuum in the heart of every man which cannot be filled by any created thing, but only by God, the Creator, made known through Jesus." [4]

VANCOUVER, BRITISH COLUMBIA, 1994 A.D.

Post-modern Canadian novelist Douglas Coupland concludes his book *Life After God*:

> My secret is that I need God—that I am sick and can no longer make it alone. I need God to help me give, because I no longer seem to be capable of giving; to help me be kind, as I no longer seem capable of kindness; to help me love, as I seem beyond being able to love. [5]

Four continents. Three millennia. Same longing. It's a universal desire, crossing all boundaries of time and geography: *We thirst for God.* You're dry without Him, soul-parched.

But God doesn't just want to give you a *drink*. God wants to get you *drenched*.

RUN THROUGH THE SPRINKLERS

Remember how great it felt when you were a kid, and on a hot summer day you'd run through the sprinklers? It was fun to get totally soaked.

The Apostle Paul has an intriguingly liquid description of what it's like to know God. He tells the Ephesians that he prays for them to *"know this love that surpasses knowledge—that you may be filled to the measure of all the fullness of God."* (EPHESIANS 3:19)

Day 1: God Thirst

The phrase he uses, *"filled to the measure of all the fullness,"* conjures pictures of a cup overflowing with cool drink, or a piece of dirty cloth saturated with cleansing water. Or a kid racing through sprinklers. It means to be soaked in God.

Doesn't that sound good to you?

I've been soaked in anger.

I've been soaked in lust.

I've been soaked in sorrow and soaked in worries.

Now I long to be *soaked* in God, to be immersed in thoughts of His love and power and presence. I want to be dripping wet.

It's interesting that Paul prays this specifically for the Ephesian Christians, of all people. The Bible says they were a church known for their hard work, their good deeds — but they had fallen away from their first love (see Revelation 2). They had apparently lost their child-like delight in their Father's affection. Their faith was parched and dry.

But Paul doesn't lecture or scold them. Instead he prays for them to get filled to the brim. To be saturated with wonder. Immersed in love.

They needed a good *soaking*. Why?

GET DRENCHED

If you've ever longed to be closer to your Creator…

If you've ever wondered if God loves you (or *still* loves you, after what you've done)…

Day 1: God Thirst

If you've felt lately like there is something vital missing from your spiritual life…

It's time to get drenched.

As you continue in this study, spend some quality time running through the sprinklers each day.

HOW TO MAKE IT IMMERSIVE

1. *Use This Book with **The** Book:* I *strongly* encourage you to keep a Bible right next to this book, and *read those passages daily*. That will change a quick devotional time into a real refreshing *soaking*. If you don't have a Bible, you can get one free at a local church, download free Bible apps, or use the free on-line Bibles at sites like www.biblegateway.com.

2. *Use This Book with Music:* There is just something about good music that turns *theology* into *experience*. I put a suggested soundtrack to this study in the back of this book. Make some of these songs into a playlist on your iPod or CD player. Soak in it throughout these 50 days.

3. *Use This Book with Others:* After each day's readings there are questions to help you interact with the material. Keep a notebook nearby to record your answers. If you can, share your responses with others: Friends, family, small group members. You can use the discussion starter videos on our web site (www.tlc.org/GodIs). To help, there are small group guides at the back of the book.

The point is, *immerse yourself* in God-thoughts. And mull those thoughts over throughout the day.

Day 1: God Thirst

The really great news is this: *You have a God-thirst precisely because there is a God who wants to pour Himself into your life.* If you open yourself to Him, it will happen! Expect to be filled to the brim with all the fullness of God!

God is… ready to get you soaked! ~~bathed~~

QUESTIONS FOR REFLECTION:

Does getting "God-soaked" sound good to you? Why or why not?

How does your soul feel?

- Dry and parched

- Enduring a drought but rain clouds are on the horizon

- It's a dry season but there are still waterholes here and there

- The rivers are flowing but the land needs irrigating

- Luxuriant, verdant, soaked with a sense of God's love

How do you see people trying to quench their "God-thirst" apart from God? How have you tried to do that?

— sexually
— shopping
— food
but also a life-thirst

THE LAUNCH

READ YOUR BIBLE: *Isaiah 40:1–9*

SPOTLIGHT VERSE: *Make straight in the desert a highway for our God. Every valley shall be exalted and every mountain and hill brought low... The glory of the* LORD *shall be revealed.* ISAIAH 40:3B–5A (NKJV)

IN BILL MOYERS' BOOK *A World of Ideas: Part Two*, a man named Joseph Needleman remembers:

> I was an observer at the launch of Apollo 17. It was a night launch, and there were hundreds of cynical reporters all over the lawn, drinking beer, wisecracking, waiting for the 35-story rocket.
>
> The countdown came. Then the launch.
>
> The first thing you see is this extraordinary light, which is just at the limit of what you can bear to look at. Everything is illuminated with this light. Then comes this thing slowly rising up in total silence, because it takes a few seconds for the sound

13

to come across. You hear a *'WHOOOOOSH!
HHHHMMMM!'* It enters right into you.

You can practically hear jaws dropping. The sense of
wonder fills everyone in the place as this thing goes
up and up. It becomes like a star, but you realize
there are humans on it.

And then there's total silence.

People just get up quietly, helping each other. They're
kind, they open doors. They look at one another,
speaking quietly and interestedly. These were
suddenly moral people because the sense of wonder,
the experience of wonder, had made them moral. [6]

Something like that happens when you study God; the
wonder changes you.

In the bright light of God you see your own fragility — and
that perspective produces in you a good kind of fear,
something like the awe of the reporters witnessing the
Saturn rocket launch.

Did you check out today's reading? Isaiah paints a picture of
the glory of God leveling mountains. He says that before the
glory of God, *"all people are like grass."*

You feel so small.

You know He is so big.

Behold your God.

Day 2: The Launch

[handwritten: I pray for patience at home, in the car, getting thru the list of personal demands]

BLOWN AWAY BY GOD

In a verse I quoted yesterday, the Apostle Paul prays for the Christians in Ephesus to know God. But Paul uses a fascinating expression. He prays that they would *"know this love that surpasses knowledge."* (EPHESIANS 3:19)

But how can you *know* something that *surpasses knowledge?*

It happened with the reporters and the rocket, didn't it? They might have known the technical details of rocket *science*. But whatever knowledge level they had was swamped by the experience of the rocket *launch*.

That's exactly my prayer for you during this study—not just that you learn stuff you didn't know before, but that the bone-shaking rumble and roar of the God-rocket fills your chest, your heart, and your soul… and that this experience has results far beyond awe.

[handwritten: I'm falling for you // a propos]

KNOWLEDGE THAT TRANSFORMS

Like the reporters who were moved by their sense of wonder to help each other, you and I too become changed when in awe of God.

You'll see.

So get ready for something that will rock your world.

Something that will illuminate everything with light, that will enter right into you, that will create a new sense of healthy fear where perhaps none existed before. And a new sense of being loved where perhaps none existed either.

[handwritten: What is purpose? more to a c to m.]

15

LET YOURSELF BE VULNERABLE

All you have to do? Psalm 46:10 says, *"Be still and know that I am God."* The phrase "Be still" means *relax.* In Hebrew it literally means to "let your arms down to your side"—to be vulnerable to God.

During this study, can you calm down long enough to *know God?* Can you "be still" and let your guard down—and without defensiveness, be open and vulnerable to what God wants to show you?

Because this study will be less about you examining God than about God examining *you.*

Learning about the attributes of God is not about putting God in a box...

it's about realizing God does not fit in the box you have Him in.

it's about encountering God as wild and free and full of fierce love.

it's about the roar of the rocket and the whisper of His love.

Are you ready?

QUESTIONS FOR REFLECTION:

What are you looking forward to most as you enter this study? *PEACE. Internal peace.*

In what way are you struggling with being still? *? nothing*

What is it that you are most defensive about—where do you know you should change, yet least want to change?

16

CHATTING WITH EINSTEIN

READ YOUR BIBLE: *Isaiah 40:10–31*

SPOTLIGHT VERSE: *"To whom will you compare me? Who is my equal?" says the Holy One.* ISAIAH 40:25

IN HIS FAMOUS ESSAY *"Thinking as a Hobby,"* William Golding writes about his surprise when, as an 18-year-old student at Oxford, he ran into Albert Einstein.

> I was looking over a small bridge in Magdalen Deer Park, and a tiny mustached and hatted figure came and stood by my side... Einstein.

> But Professor Einstein knew no English at that time and I knew only two words of German. I beamed at him, trying wordlessly to convey by my bearing all the affection and respect that the English felt for him... yet I doubt if my face conveyed more than a formless awe. I would have given my Greek and Latin and French and a good slice of my English for enough German to communicate. But we were

divided; he was …inscrutable. For perhaps five minutes we stood together on the bridge, undeniable grade-one thinker and breathless aspirant. With true greatness, Professor Einstein realized that any contact was better than none. He pointed to a trout wavering in midstream.

He spoke: "Fisch."

My brain reeled. Here I was, mingling with the great, and yet helpless… Desperately I sought for some sign by which I might convey that I, too, revered pure reason. I nodded vehemently. In a brilliant flash I used up half of my German vocabulary. "Fisch. Ja. Ja."

Then Professor Einstein, his whole figure still conveying good will and amiability, drifted away out of sight. [7]

Is that what it's like to encounter God?

You long to convey affection and respect, and you want so badly to hear from Him, but is there just too great a gap between your brain and His greatness? You revere Him. But He drifts away, out of sight.

The Bible does say that God is unfathomable:

> *Who can fathom the Spirit of the LORD,*
> *or instruct the LORD as his counselor?*
> *…Surely the nations are like a drop in a bucket;*
> *they are regarded as dust on the scales;*
> *he weighs the islands as though they were fine dust.*

Day 3: Chatting with Einstein

*…He sits enthroned above the circle of the earth,
and its people are like grasshoppers.* ISAIAH 40:13, 15, 22A

*"For my thoughts are not your thoughts, neither are
your ways my ways," declares the* LORD. ISAIAH 55:8

KNOWING THE UNKNOWABLE GOD

Science fiction writer H.G. Wells wrote a story about a pastor and an angel in conversation.

The angel tells the pastor the obvious: "You don't fully understand the truth about God."

The pastor desperately responds, "But the truth—you can tell me the truth!"

And the angel smiles and lovingly strokes the bald spot on the pastor's head. "Truth?" he says. "Yes, I could tell you. But could this hold it? Not this little box of brains." [8]

How can my "little box of brains" ever hold the truth about God? How can I hope to know *anything* about a Being so immense, so beyond my comprehension, so different from me?

The Bible's answer: *I can't.*

I can't even imagine I know *anything* about God.

Unless…

Unless *God tells me.*

Unless God chooses to reveal Himself to me in terms I can understand. Unless that happens, everything I think about

God is potentially an idol, a building of God in my own image.

The really good news is, *that is exactly what God does.* He is, as theologians put it, *self-revelatory.* He reveals Himself.

GOD UNVEILS HIMSELF

> *He who forms the mountains,*
> *who creates the wind,*
> *and **who reveals his thoughts to mankind,***
> *who turns dawn to darkness,*
> *and treads on the heights of the earth —*
> *the* LORD *God Almighty is his name.* AMOS 4:13

God reveals his thoughts to *me?*

This should instill in me a sense of awe and humility as I move into any study of God. *I can only know about God because He chooses to let me know.*

Why? Why does God do that? What is man, that God is mindful of him?

Well, God is not only perfect in power; He is perfect in love. He is not only infinite in *perfection* but infinite in *affection.*

So God's goal in letting me know about Himself is not just for me to know His *power* (or to impress others with my knowledge), but for me to know His *love.*

LOVE IS THE AGENDA

I like the way Margaret Feinberg puts it: "Some say that love has no agenda, but... I have come to believe that love *is* the agenda." [9]

Love is the reason for God's self-revelation. God *longs* to be known by you, even more than you long to know God.

Think of God's increasingly intimate self-revelation out of love for you and me:

There are clues to God everywhere in nature. Because God loves you, He speaks to you in leaves and stars and babies and bears and waves and mountains and storms and sunsets and more. It's what theologians call *general revelation* (creation).

> *God's glory is on tour in the skies, God-craft on exhibit across the horizon.* PSALM 19:1A (THE MESSAGE)

But God desires your *love*, not just your distant, frightened respect for His greatness. So He also speaks to you in poems and stories and letters and songs and prophecies, recorded in the Bible. It's what theologians call *special revelation* (Scripture).

You might guess He's *great* by looking at nature, but you learn He's *loving* by reading the Bible.

What's more, *special* revelation gives you a very cool lens through which to see *general* revelation. When you see the world made by God through the lens of the word inspired by God, wonders abound all around. You perceive His Nature revealed in nature, His Beauty behind all beauty, the Creator in creation.

So God reveals Himself to us in nature and in His Word. Then the two come together: The Word comes into the world. Jesus is born.

The Word became flesh and made his dwelling among us. JOHN 1:14A

At the incarnation, God's nature exists with human nature. In Jesus Christ I see who God is more clearly than ever before.

God keeps self-revealing, closer and closer.

THE IMPORTANCE OF INCOMPREHENSIBILITY

Don't get me wrong. To say

God is self-revelatory doesn't mean

God is easy to understand.

He is, after all,

God.

He exists far beyond any category I could ever put Him in.

In fact, if I am learning about the true God, I should expect to be blown away pretty regularly with thoughts that stagger my imagination (The idea that He is "three-yet-one," for example). I'm pretty sure that if I fully comprehend everything in a study about God, I'm not really studying the incomprehensible God!

But God can give me a knowledge of Himself that is *real*, even if I can't fully wrap my head around it.

I can *know* something *beyond knowledge*, as Paul says. I can taste a berry and *know* its goodness without knowing precisely how to describe it.

Day 3: Chatting with Einstein

This study is not about dissecting God into pieces you can analyze. Because, really, good luck if you want to try to analyze God like that.

It's about tasting, and seeing, that the Lord is good.

PRAYING FOR EYES TO SEE

To know God *that* way I really do need more than my little box of brains. I have to pray that God opens the eyes of my heart.

This is why Paul also says to the Ephesians,

> *"I pray that the eyes of your heart may be enlightened in order that you may know... his incomparably great power..."* EPHESIANS 1:18A, 19A

During this 50-day study, I suggest you pray this:

"Lord, may the same Spirit who inspired the Word enlighten *me.*"

Then keep those eyes wide open.

You are not only going to find your mind blown—you are going to find your heart filled. Because He loves you,

God is... revealing Himself to you right now.

QUESTIONS FOR REFLECTION:

When people do not believe God is self-revelatory, how might their relationship with God be affected negatively?

How will thinking that God is self-revelatory have a positive impact on your thoughts, emotions, and actions?

You might agree that, in theory, God is self-revelatory. But does your life demonstrate that you really believe this?

How might your daily actions change if you really focused on and believed this attribute of God?

MEETING THE OTHER

READ YOUR BIBLE: *Isaiah 6:1–8*

SPOTLIGHT VERSE: *Holy, holy, holy is the Lord Almighty; the whole earth is full of his glory.* ISAIAH 6:3B

I WAS RAISED IN California by immigrant parents from Switzerland, and my Swiss heritage was a matter of deep personal pride for me as a kid.

Then the summer after I turned 16, I did an internship at a radio station in Switzerland. And something amazing happened.

I was surprised by a call from our station manager.

The President of Switzerland would be visiting our studios to broadcast his annual Swiss Independence Day message to the nation!

I was so excited, and dressed in such a hurry, that I forgot to put on deodorant—an oversight that turned out to really matter when, after his radio address, the President turned to me and asked me out to dinner with his family, right then and there!

I remember thinking, "Is this a weird dream? Is the President really asking me to dinner *on the only day all year I have forgotten deodorant?*"

But it was no dream. And believe me, I smelled terrible.

I said, "Yes."

Then I started strategizing: "I'll order fondue and blame the odor on the cheese!" For the rest of the night I moved my arms only from the elbows forward, pinning my underarms as tightly to my torso as possible.

That only meant that I proceeded to really stink up the place (a nervous 16-year-old boy with no deodorant! Imagine!) while simultaneously gesturing freakishly. I tried to keep my distance from the Great Man … but then… the President beckoned me to sit right next to his place at the table!

In that moment I was alternately more delighted and more dismayed than I'd ever been in my life: "The President is asking me to sit at his right hand! Yes! I smell like a pickup truck full of wet dogs! Nooooo!"

A jittery chef prepared our meals tableside while he took nervous glances at the president. For one of the courses the chef poured brandy over some fancy food item I did not recognize, the idea apparently being that he would then set it on fire to create a spectacular display. Only he was shaking so badly that he poured out a little too much, and when he lit the dish, a giant fireball suddenly whooshed into the air making me even more nervous than I was before!

Yet to put me at ease the President graciously asked me questions about my life the whole evening. I kept calling him "H-H-Herr P-P-P-President" until he insisted I call him "Kurt."

Eventually, though I knew I did not belong in the picture, I was soothed by his graciousness and truly enjoyed my meal—and have been looking for openings to tell people about my brush with Swiss greatness ever since!

MEETING THE RULER OF EVERYTHING

I think of that story when I read Isaiah 6, because something like that—but on an infinitely greater cosmic scale, of course—was experienced by the prophet Isaiah.

He was an advisor to kings who lived about 700 years before Christ. So, unlike me, Isaiah was used to being around heads of state. An aristocrat. Not easily intimidated.

Yet he falls flat on his face when he suddenly sees the throne of God. And what happens next gives great insight into the mystery of the Divine.

Isaiah realizes how much his sin must stink in the presence of such holiness. He despairs,

> *"Woe to me! I am ruined! For I am a man of unclean lips, and I live among a people of unclean lips, and my eyes have seen the King, the* LORD *Almighty."* ISAIAH 6:5

What prompted that kind of response?

EARTH-SHAKING HOLINESS

Here's what Isaiah saw: Seraphim (angelic beings), were calling out in temple-rattling voices:

> *"Holy, holy, holy is the* L**ORD** *Almighty; the whole earth is full of his glory."*

Why do they repeat the word "holy" three times?

Well, when the Bible reiterates a word, it's like God is circling it, underlining it, highlighting it.

As Max Lucado says, "God is not just holy. Or holy holy. God is *holy holy holy.*" [10]

The Hebrew word for "holy" is *qadosh*, which means *totally separate*. It has two meanings related to God:

OTHER OTHER OTHER

First, *qadosh* means God is totally *other*. God is so different, so separate, so unlike you and me that He is *other, other, other*.

Why emphasize this?

Because although the Bible says God made us in His image, we've been trying to make God in our image ever since.

Go to a museum. Look at any ancient idol. It may have been crafted in sincere hope, but you always learn more about the people who made it than you do about God. The Egyptian gods look like Egyptians, the Sumerian gods like Sumerians.

And what about our God?

Day 4: Meeting the Other

Garrison Keillor, famous for his Lake Woebegone stories, tells of an anonymous complaint nailed to the door of the local church:

> You have taught me to worship a god who is like you, who shares your thinking exactly, who is going to slap me one if I don't straighten out fast. I am very uneasy every Sunday, which is cloudy and deathly still and filled with silent accusing whispers. [11]

I need a God bigger than that. Bigger than your ideas of God. Bigger than mine.

In his classic book *Your God Is Too Small*, J. B. Phillips describes how the world sees many Christians:

> If they are not strenuously defending an outgrown conception of God, then they are cherishing a hothouse God who could only exist between the pages of a Bible or between the four walls of a church. [12]

As Ana-Maria Rizzuto observed, "No child arrives at the house of God without his pet God under his arm." [13]

That's why I need to remind myself continually that the real God rattles the foundation of any church. I don't have God figured out. Or tamed. He is not my pet. He is beyond any limitations.

This is a good thing. God is not constrained by my fears or my imagination. It is a relief to know: God is *totally other*.

PURE PURE PURE

Then there's another level of meaning to *qadosh*: God is *totally pure.*

God is not contaminated by impurity or sin at any level.

He is *pure, pure, pure.*

What's the point of that?

Again, look at the ideas of God held by other cultures during Isaiah's time: You see deities infected by envy, pettiness, grudges, pride, lust... because if you create God in your own image you'll magnify not only your powers, but your short-comings as well.

The repetition of the word "holy" is meant to convey that God has none of those moral flaws.

So the word *holy* indicates that God is totally *other* and totally pure, the one who sets up all the rules, writes all the definitions, creates all the standards. Any true encounter with Him is always on His terms.

UNWORTHY ME

Isaiah declares that he is unworthy to stand before such a *qadosh, qadosh, qadosh* Being.

And he *is* unworthy.

God never says, "No, Isaiah, you're the man! You're totally my equal, absolutely worthy to stand alongside me."

Instead... *God cleanses him.* What Isaiah needs is not a self-esteem boost. He needs pardon. Forgiveness. New life.

One of the seraphim flies to Isaiah with a coal from the altar which he touches to Isaiah's lips as he says, *"Behold… your iniquity is taken away and your sin is forgiven."*

Then God asks for someone to be His ambassador to the people, and Isaiah, rejuvenated by the fact that God has cleansed him, immediately says, *"Here am I. Send me!"*

And God does.

THE RHYTHM OF A GOD-ENCOUNTER

This is always the rhythm of any true encounter with the *holy, holy, holy* God.

First, there is an awestruck awareness of my own unworthiness.

Then there is a reaching out to me, from God. He is the one who extends grace to me while I am flat on my face, as good as dead.

And then…

Then I want to go and tell the world about what a great God I have met!

My message becomes all about God, not about me: I have received His grace and so I cannot stop telling others about my experience.

Kind of like the day I went to dinner with the President:

When you think of God you might become uncomfortable, aware of how much you must stink in His presence, even on your best day. I think that's what people mean when they say, "If I ever walked into church, the building would collapse!"

That's an understandable emotion.

But God is the one who says, "Now that you see my holiness, let me cleanse you. And then deputize you."

After I encounter the totally *different* God, I am *different*.

The *Pure One* purifies *me*.

The *Other One* makes *me* into another.

Meeting the *qadosh* God makes me *qadosh* too.

God is... *Other*.

QUESTIONS FOR REFLECTION:

How does the story in Isaiah 6:1–8 inspire you?

Summarize what it means to you that God is *holy holy holy*:

Many people do not realize how holy God is, both in other-ness and in purity. Because of this, what unrealistic ideas do they have about God and themselves, and how do the two relate?

DAY 5
MAKING IDOLS

READ YOUR BIBLE: *Isaiah 44:6–22*

SPOTLIGHT VERSE: *Who fashions a god or casts an idol that is profitable for nothing?* ISAIAH 44:10 (ESV)

"Our premier human problem is idolatry and its consequences." —David A. Hubbard

A LOT OF CHRISTIANS seem more *pagan* than *Christian*: We get many, if not most, of our ideas about God from Greek, Roman, and Northern European mythology.

Really, when we think of an old man in heaven with a white beard throwing down lightning bolts, we're thinking of *Zeus*, not Jehovah.

Compare that to what God reveals about Himself.

Here are a few of the biblical attributes of God we'll look at in this book:

Omnipotence, meaning God is all-powerful.

Day 5: Making Idols

No matter what I face, it's never too much for God.

Omnipresence, meaning God is everywhere.

I don't have to go to a special temple or other sacred place in order to meet God.

Sovereignty, meaning God is in control.

Nothing that happens can possibly ruin God's plans.

Immutability, meaning God is unchanging.

He always keeps His promises, He is always faithful.

And one of my favorite attributes, just because it's so mind-blowing:

Aseity, meaning God is not dependent on anything for His existence. The Hebrew name God gives Himself in the Bible, *Yahweh*, is derived from the Hebrew verb meaning *"to be."* This means God simply *is.*

Everything else in the universe is contingent, or dependent on something for its existence. Except God. He is dependent on nothing.

These attributes are so unlike the god I create when left to my own devices.

Just go through some attributes on that list.

The pagan gods were not believed to be *omnipotent.*

And when I live with the unspoken fear that some things are just too big for God to work out for good, I prove I really have more of a pagan picture of God than a biblical one.

Day 5: Making Idols

They were not *sovereign*. Other gods and even people conspired to thwart their plans.

When I get the idea that God might have His plan for my life spoiled by a seeming disaster — or my own stupid moves — I'm thinking of something like an old pagan god.

They were not believed to be *immutable*. They changed their minds all the time.

And when I get insecure that God has changed *("Does God still love me?")* I betray the true origins of my theology.

I might not think I have much in common with an ancient craftsman who carved an idol. But when I worry, when I get insecure, when I feel shame, it's often because deep down, in the core of my being, it's that I have forgotten what the Bible has to say about God.

FASHION GOD?

I like the way some older translations put it: People *fashion* idols. That phrase nails it. I often make a false god that fits my fashion, or society's fashions and trends. A fashion-god.

This is especially so in our current pop culture, where, in a genuine desire for tolerance and unity, everything that sounds vaguely religious is thrown together and cooked into one big spiritual soup that blurs legitimate distinctions between theological systems. The resulting concoction often is so bland, and has so little "bite," that it's unappetizing and ineffective.

Day 5: Making Idols

We look down at the creations of our own meager imaginations while the God beyond imagining is right there next to us, ready to love and empower us.

In Acts 17, Paul is explaining this to the Greek philosophers in Athens. He says:

> ... *we should not think that the divine being is like gold or silver or stone—an image made by human design and skill.* ACTS 17:24–25,29

Paul explains further that, although God is totally different from the images we make of Him, He still preserves us and reaches out to us:

> *God did this so that they would seek him and perhaps reach out for him and find him, though he is not far from any one of us. For in him we live and move and have our being.* ACTS 17:27–28

God is all around you, waiting for you to reach out and do exactly the kind of thing we're doing in this study. He will help you. He *wants* you to linger and learn and love Him.

MEET THE ONE WHO LOVES YOU

It's intriguing to me that of all the attributes God wants the people to remember in Isaiah 44, He reminds them most often to remember this:

He is their *Redeemer.*

That's because the most damaging thing about idols is that *they can't save you.* They're powerless, not only to bring rain or fertility, but far more importantly, to bring redemption.

So God is calling you to turn away from your fashioned god to the God who Is, not just to find *truth*, but to find *life*. When you delve into the mystery of God you are exhilarated, and not just from the joy of unraveling a mystery.

You are meeting the *Other* who loves you.

God is… not an idol.

QUESTIONS FOR REFLECTION:

Which of the attributes of God discussed in today's chapter do you see yourself struggling the most to believe? How does this affect your life?

Which of the attributes do you most long to learn more about?

CHILD-LIKE WONDER

READ YOUR BIBLE: *Psalm 8*

SPOTLIGHT VERSE: *But I have stilled and quieted my soul; like a weaned child with its mother, like a weaned child is my soul within me.* PSALM 131:2 (NIV, 1984)

YES, GOD WILL BLOW your mind. Yet He communicates in ways even a child, or a childlike adult, can understand.

The infinite speaks even to infants.

I love the book *Children's Letters to God*, a collection of real notes written by kids in various Sunday School classes.[14] The sense of worship these letters often express proves to me that getting *God-soaked* meets a basic human desire:

> *Dear God: I didn't think orange went with purple until I saw the sunset you made on Tuesday. That was cool. Love, Eugene.*

> *Dear God, I think about you sometimes even when I'm not praying!*

Day 6: Child-like Wonder

Dear God: I don't ever feel alone since I found out about you.

Have you noticed how often kids think about God, and ask great questions? They're amateur theologians.

But as they get older kids often stop the God-talk. Why?

I think people slowly grow to believe that a study of God is only for the super-smart specialists. So they defer all their God thoughts to the experts. And they grow thirsty.

Maybe, if you're honest, you even feel a little under-qualified to think theologically in this study, just because you don't know all the Christian vocabulary.

THE WISDOM OF WONDER

I would love for you to meet Sarah Kritikos.

In her early 20s, Sarah's an enthusiastic regular attender at our church's class for adults with special needs, *Joyful Noise.* And she is so full of the joy of life.

But Sarah's had a lot of challenges. She was born with numerous life-threatening health problems as well as several physical and developmental difficulties.

Sarah has been in and out of hospitals at least *30 times* over the years. She stands somewhere near four feet tall and is not much bigger around than one of my legs. One of her arms is half the normal length and is missing a thumb.

I might be tempted to give up if I had those kinds of challenges. But Sarah knows something about the attributes of God. Because, even if she doesn't call them by their theo-logical names, she thinks about them. *A lot.*

I saw Sarah at a Christian camp recently. Some men were up for the day doing volunteer construction work and Sarah bounded right into the middle of their break and chatted with them. Then later in the week I got this email from one of those guys:

> Hi, my name is Ron. I met Sarah only for a moment but her impact was like a thunder clap.
>
> There was a short break before dinner. We sat down on the deck to rest—and Sarah walked by and said, "Can I ask you guys a question?"
>
> "Sure," we replied.
>
> She asked, *"What do you think is the most beautiful part of God?"*
>
> We each answered.
>
> "Can I ask you another question?" Sarah said with enthusiasm. *"When you have troubles, who do you turn to?"*
>
> We were stunned that this tiny woman with a strange delivery but beautiful smile could ask us questions that would make us grown men weep. God used her voice and He spoke directly to me. Through my experience with Sarah, I had a conversation with God. *This was my first experience like this.* Sarah truly is an instrument of God. Thank you, Sarah!

Day 6: Child-like Wonder

I think I know the reason Sarah's been able to navigate all the crazy rapids in her young life. She really loves God — and loves to think about the One she loves.

Sarah is not what many would call sophisticated or clever. But she is full of wonder. And I'll take that over sophisticated or clever any day.

As you continue this study of God's attributes, don't be intimidated by it. And don't keep it academic. Think about the difference it makes at every turn, like Sarah does.

God is so loving that He reveals Himself with gentleness and patience despite anyone's apparent weaknesses. *In His self-revelation to you, God is not limited by any of your limitations.* Isn't that an awesome thought?

But you must have a willingness to wonder. Like Sarah.

Ask yourself her wise question:

"What do you think is the most beautiful part of God?"

God is… eager for you to know Him!

QUESTION FOR REFLECTION:
What do you think is the most beautiful part of God?

PERSPECTIVE SHIFT

READ YOUR BIBLE: *Psalm 100*

SPOTLIGHT VERSE: *Know that the LORD is God. It is he who made us, and we are his; we are his people, the sheep of his pasture.* PSALM 100:3

IN MAX LUCADO'S BOOK *It's Not About Me* he describes the Copernican Revolution:

> Until Copernicus came along in 1543, we earthlings enjoyed center stage. Fathers could place an arm around their children, point to the night sky, and proclaim, "The universe revolves around us." [15]

He goes on to point out how for centuries, earth was thought to be the hub of the wheel in the sky, the center of the solar system. All the other planets revolved around... us!

Then along came Copernicus.

He pointed to the sun and said, "Behold the center of our system."

No one wanted to hear it.

His book was immediately placed on the papal index of forbidden books. When Galileo later said the same thing, the king locked him up and the church kicked him out.

But he was right. And his new, accurate perspective changed everything, explained so much and put us in our proper place.

Well, as Lucado says, "What Copernicus did for the solar system, God does for our souls." [16]

A study of God reveals the truth:

I am not the center of the universe in any sense.

I am not the star of the show.

I am not in charge.

This is one of the healthiest results of a study of the attributes of God. But this new, accurate perspective is resisted by the medieval monarch of my soul: *Me.*

NOT NUMBER ONE

The ugly truth is, I *want* to be the center of the universe. I want to be in charge. I want to look out for number one.

I do not like it when I am told that my default mode—wanting the weather and the traffic and the economy and my kids and my spouse and my cat and my church and my whole world to suit my wishes—is not reality. I like to live in denial of this, imprisoning the messenger instead of considering the message.

But the Bible reminds me:

> *Know that the* LORD *is God. It is he who made us, and we are his; we are his people, the sheep of his pasture.* PSALM 100:3

I love the way the Psalmist orients me to the true center of the universe in that verse:

Know that the LORD *is God.*

Not me.

It is He who made us.

Not we who made Him.

We are His.

Not our own.

We are His people, the sheep of His pasture.

Not the other way around.

That's hard for us humans to really get. To quote Anne Lamott, "The biggest difference between you and God is that God doesn't think He's you." [17]

Try this as a helpful exercise: Take your index finger and point up and say out loud: "God." Now point at yourself and say: "Not." Repeat as necessary.

This is important to remember for your own sanity.

NOT GOD

Ernest Kurtz wrote a history of the 12-step movement. It's called *Not God*.[18]

Healing and recovery, he says, begins with a single realization: I am not God. I need help from a power *greater than myself*.

And then, when you read the Bible's teaching that this same God, awesome in power...

chooses to show love

and bring healing

and reveal Himself

to *you*

something happens.

Something people call worship, or release, or freedom. Whatever you call that encounter, you are changed. Because you have met God. And He is not you.

God is... not me.

QUESTIONS FOR REFLECTION:

In what ways do people sometimes show that they expect to be the center of their universe?

In what ways do you do this?

Why is it important to realize that God is God, and you are not? How can this help your life?

GOD IS

Majestic
Omnipotent
Awesome

The greatest single distinguishing feature of the omnipotence of God is that our imagination gets lost when thinking about it. BLAISE PASCAL

IS YOUR GOD TOO SMALL?

READ YOUR BIBLE: *Psalm 29*

SPOTLIGHT VERSE: *The voice of the Lord is powerful; the voice of the Lord is majestic.* PSALM 29:4

IN THE CHURCH WHERE I was raised, we talked a lot about God being *personal.* But in retrospect, this seemed to give some people the idea that they could have their own *personal god,* meaning a god that fit their idea of what a god should be like.

I can do that too. As I mentioned earlier, one of my big temptations is to create a little mental idol, a false godlet made in my own image, a deity that approves of all my indulgences and gets angry with everything I'm peeved about too.

God is *personal,* but that doesn't mean He's a person *like me.* The Bible talks a lot about God's bigness and otherness, or, to use a more biblical term, *majesty.*

The Bible writers loved that word.

> *The LORD reigns, he is robed in majesty;*
> *the LORD is robed in majesty and armed with*
> *strength...* PSALM 93:1A

48

Day 8: Is Your God Too Small?

They speak of the glorious splendor of your
majesty — and I will meditate on your wonderful
works. PSALM 145:5

Our English word "majesty" comes from Latin; it means *greatness*. This is what the Bible means when it talks about God being "on high" and "in heaven." It doesn't mean He lives up there, in space, or is physically above you, but that He is far above you in greatness, and is worthy to be adored and worshipped.

And feared.

IS YOUR GOD TOO TAME?

It's interesting that when people in the Bible encounter God, their first reaction is always the same: Fear. Not always a cringing, shameful fear, either; many times it's appropriate awe and reverence and gasping wonder at encountering the most majestic Being in the universe.

This is so healthy. The Bible says,

The fear of the LORD is the beginning of wisdom:
and the knowledge of the holy is understanding.
PROVERBS 9:10 (KJV)

Maybe this is an aspect of God we miss in our culture because our thinking about God is so anemic; we hardly ever think about Him, and when we do, we think of one of our little godlets we fashion, and not the might and majesty of the actual God.

Maybe this is also why we can sin so blithely. In the Old Testament, one phrase repeatedly describes people who

49

pursue destructive behavior: *"there was no fear of God before their eyes."*

In C.S. Lewis' classic *The Lion, the Witch, and the Wardrobe*, one of the children asks Mr. and Mrs. Beaver about Aslan, the great king and lion:

> "Is Aslan quite safe? I shall feel rather nervous about meeting a lion."

> "That you will dearie, and no mistake," said Mrs. Beaver. "If there's anyone who can appear before Aslan without their knees knocking, they're either braver than most or just plain silly."

> "Then he isn't safe?" said Lucy.

> "Safe?" said Mr. Beaver; "don't you hear what Mrs. Beaver tells you? Who said anything about safe? 'Course he isn't safe. But he's good. He's the King, I tell you." [19]

Is God safe?

Well, He is our Savior, our Refuge, our Rock. So He is *good*.

But if *safe* means that God never does anything I dislike, that God always meets my puny expectations, that God is never alarming, then, no, He's definitely not safe.

God is wild, majestic, mighty, creative, challenging…

In Mark Buchanan's book *Is Your God Too Safe?* he says:

> The safe god asks nothing of us, gives nothing to us. He never makes us bold to dance… never whispers

anything in our ears but greeting card slogans… a safe god inspires neither awe, nor worship, nor sacrifice… [20]

Is your God too safe? Good question!

POWER SOURCE

That's why, for the next several days, we'll be focusing on what you could call the *majestic* attributes of God. After this I hope your knees knock some when you think of Him.

Let's start by looking at the *omnipotence* of God, from the words *omni* meaning *all*, and *potence*, meaning *power*. When theologians say God is *omnipotent* they mean He is *all-powerful*.

When you first see God in the Bible, in Genesis 1, He's creating everything you and I know—time, space, the earth, and all life. So, chronologically and logically, God's creative power seems like a good place to start a study of God's attributes.

In today's reading in Psalm 29, David is trying to capture the power and majesty of God by comparing Him to the fury and might of a storm. The power of God in these verses is wild, untamed, frightening.

But check out the surprise ending:

> *The Lord gives strength to his people;*
> *the Lord blesses his people with peace.* PSALM 29:11

I love that David *ends* with that. Because after you've seen God's power, His offer of strength makes a lifelong impression.

Facing a problem that makes you feel weak and powerless? Remind yourself that God is infinitely more powerful than the problem you are facing right now. Asking Him for strength will not dilute his reservoir of power in any way. And you will be *"blessed with peace."*

In prayer today, say, "God, You're all powerful. Nothing is too hard for You. With God all things are possible. You rule over nations. You rule over nature. You rule the universe. And You give me strength and bless me with peace."

God is... majestic.

QUESTIONS FOR REFLECTION:

In what ways do people sometimes have a God that is "too safe"?

What are the most impressive displays of nature's power you have witnessed? How do these displays remind you about God's power?

What is the promise in Psalm 29:11? What situation are you facing where you need to claim that promise?

DAY 9
THE MIRACLE OF LIFE

READ YOUR BIBLE: *Psalm 33:1–9*

SPOTLIGHT VERSE: *By the word of the* LORD *the heavens were made, their starry host by the breath of his mouth.* PSALM 33:6

FOR THE NEXT FEW days I want to help you to rediscover wonder.

To get lost in amazement.

To wander in worship.

Famous scientist Stephen Hawking wrote *The Grand Design* to defend his atheism. Ironically, the book had the exact opposite effect on me: It rocketed my faith in the creativity and omnipotence of God to new heights. For weeks after reading just the first chapter I walked around in wide-eyed wonder that anything living existed at all.

In that first chapter Hawking says, "The discovery recently of the extreme fine-tuning of so many laws of nature could

53

lead some to the idea that this grand design is the work of some grand Designer..." And then he elaborates on some apparent evidences of design:

> Many improbable occurrences conspired to create Earth's human-friendly design. We need liquid water to exist, and if the Earth were too close [to the sun], it would all boil off; if it were too far, it would freeze.

> Even a small disturbance in gravity would send the planet off its circular orbit, and cause it to spiral either into or away from the sun.

> It is not only the peculiar characteristics of our solar system that seem oddly conducive to the development of human life, but also the characteristics of our entire universe — and its laws. They appear to have a design that is both tailor-made to support us and, if we are to exist, leaves little room for alteration. [21]

He goes on to produce many examples, and then concludes:

> Most of the laws of nature appear fine-tuned in the sense that if they were altered by only modest amounts, the universe would be ...unsuitable for the development of life. They do seem tailor-made for humans... [22]

In fact, he says, if you try to explain how this all happened by accident, you run into literally impossible odds. There is simply not a chance that this happened by chance!

But then Hawking goes on to handle the problem of God this way: Since it is too incredible to believe this finely-tuned *universe* came about by random chance, why not postulate an infinite number of *multiverses?*

If nature randomly spat out an infinite number of universes so that a nearly infinite number of them now exist in a multiverse, then surely at least *one* would have our characteristics, just by luck of the draw.

Another famous scientist, Paul Davies, wrote his response to this idea in the *New York Times*:

> The multiverse theory is increasingly popular, but it doesn't so much explain the laws of physics as dodge the whole issue. There has to be a physical mechanism to make all those universes and bestow bylaws on them. Where do *they* come from? The problem has simply been shifted up a level from the laws of the universe to the meta-laws of the multiverse. [23]

I am certainly not qualified to issue some detailed critique of the work of an esteemed scientist. What I get out of this debate goes in a different direction:

Everything I can see on earth every day that is alive, even common things like leaves and skin and blades of grass, is, when seen in the scope of the whole universe, more precious than the rarest jewel.

The odds against *anything* being alive *anywhere* in this universe are so great that the mere fact that you are reading these words, inhaling air, conscious of the beauty around us, thinking about this together, is less likely than you winning every lottery in history.

Day 9: *The Miracle of Life*

The Bible's explanation? God is the creative powerhouse behind everything, the artist-engineer-poet-scientist who wove it all together. The creation sparkles with life endowed by the Creator!

> *In the beginning you laid the foundations of the earth, and the heavens are the work of your hands.*
> PSALM 102:25

> *By the word of the LORD the heavens were made, their starry host by the breath of his mouth.* PSALM 33:6

And you want a real-mind-blower? The One who made all this is the One who loves you so much He gave Himself to you in Christ!

Take some precious moments today to consider the sheer greatness of God's power. Let your spirit soar with His Spirit.

Pause to see... with eyes wide open.

Take in the heavens, the stars, the moon and the sun and the clouds and the oceans and the mountains.

God is... infinitely powerful.

QUESTIONS FOR REFLECTION:

How does meditating on the omnipotence of God impact you?

Where today did you see evidence of the power of God?

AMAZING ARTIST, BRILLIANT ENGINEER

READ YOUR BIBLE: *Psalm 148*

SPOTLIGHT VERSE: *Let them praise the name of the* LORD, *for at his command they were created.* PSALM 148:5

WE WENT BIG YESTERDAY, thinking of the cosmos. Today let's go small.

Remember the old Disneyland ride *Adventure Through Inner Space* where you were "shrunk" to the size of a molecule? Well, try to imagine that actually happening. Let's say you decreased in size a billion times, until a single human cell looked as big as a city the size of New York.

Dr. Michael Denton, quoted in Jerry Bridges' book *The Joy of Fearing God*, describes what you'd see: On the surface there are millions of portholes, opening and closing to allow a stream of materials flowing in and out. You enter one of these openings and discover "a world of supreme technology and bewildering complexity":

Day 10: Amazing Artist, Brilliant Engineer

> You see endless highly organized corridors and
> conduits branching in every direction, some leading
> to the central memory bank in the nucleus and
> others to assembly plants and processing units... a
> huge range of products and raw materials shuttle
> along in orderly fashion to and from all the various
> assembly plants in the outer regions of the cell...
> [like] an immense automated factory, a factory larger
> than a city and carrying out almost as many unique
> functions as all the manufacturing activities of man
> on earth. [24]

In at least one respect it would be different from a factory,
though: "It would be capable of replicating its entire
structure within a few hours."

Now consider that there are about 75 trillion of these cells
in your body!

What does all this have to do with the power of God?

As Jerry Bridges points out, it's just one illustration of
millions that could be drawn from nature to show how God
is an amazingly creative artist and brilliant engineer.

God is like the ultimate Leonardo Da Vinci, an artist and
engineer—or I should say, Da Vinci reflected this aspect of
the image of God. And when you create art, or engineer a
solution, or do math, you do too!

We looked upward yesterday at the stars. Take time to
stop today and look more closely at the tiny world around
you. Where do you see the brilliance of God's power
displayed—just with your naked eye, never mind the

microscope it would take to unlock the wonders we just described?

Pause to see… with eyes wide open.

Take in the flowers. Butterflies. Dogs. Cats. Babies. Leaves. Water droplets. Blades of grass. The rise and fall of your own rhythmic breaths.

And take in some of the creative ways that human artists, made in God's image, try to reflect all these things.

As Elizabeth Barrett Browning wrote,

> Earth's crammed with heaven,
> And every common bush afire with God;
> But only he who sees, takes off his shoes… [25]

God is… infinitely creative.

QUESTIONS FOR REFLECTION:

How does Psalm 148 impact you?

What did you praise God for today—something you noticed in the world around you for which you have rarely given Him thanks, perhaps one of the "smaller" things?

Why is seeing the world in this way a good habit?

DAY 11
RECOVERING WONDER

READ YOUR BIBLE: *Psalm 19:1–6*

SPOTLIGHT VERSE: *The heavens proclaim the glory of God. The skies display his craftsmanship. Day after day they continue to speak; night after night they make him known.* PSALM 19:1–2 (NLT)

THE CREATOR DELIGHTS IN His creation.

The Bible says that when God created the world, He paused and said, *"It is good."* And when I get lost in wonder while enjoying His handiwork, I am reflecting His own delight.

We live in Santa Cruz, California, where I sometimes jog on an oceanfront trail that winds through Natural Bridges State Beach. Each winter, thousands of monarch butterflies migrate from Mexico to hang out there. I mean, they literally hang out, clustering like bunches of bananas from the trees, occasionally breaking free of the group to flutter across the path.

Day 11: Recovering Wonder

I enjoy running through the grove they inhabit on my way
to the beach, seeing them, and other parts of creation,
bursting with life all around me. I wish I could take you on
a run with me. Just imagine:

It's a warm day and they float around you,
like something from a dream,
delicate orange-and-black origami come to life.

At the same beach, framed by a rock arch, you watch
comical shore birds race the waves on stick-thin legs

while elegant pelicans glide just above them,
dinosaur silhouettes against the pale blue sky

In the tide pools underfoot: other glimpses of life.
Purple and red sea stars, the world's slowest predators,
advance nonchalantly on their prey;
hermit crabs scuttle sideways
carrying their stolen homes
looking for a place to lurk;
sea anemones wave their tentacles,
raising multiple hands to warn "I'm hungry!"

And then suddenly
you catch a distant glimpse:
A spout of water. A glistening fin.
Migrating whales frolic further offshore.

You look back over your shoulder and smile as you see
the fluttering butterflies that sparked your reverie
still drifting and glimmering
and the symmetry fascinates:
The minuscule monarchs and the massive whales,
mysteriously mirroring their migrations.

The other day, because I was looking for it, I saw all this *in the same hour.* Wow. My spirit was refreshed with a sense of awe. The creation was proclaiming the creativity of God pretty loudly.

Yet most days I don't notice a thing. Of course I don't. *I'm not even looking.*

As author and pastor Mark Buchanan says,

> We are all in the habit of asking the Spirit to open our minds before we read Scripture or hear a sermon. But rarely if ever do we ask the Spirit to reveal to us more of God when we study a leaf, rock, bird, child, painting, carving, or poem. [26]

This kind of wonder was certainly enjoyed by the Bible writers:

> *The heavens declare the glory of God; the skies proclaim the work of his hands.* PSALM 19:1

> *How many are your works, LORD! In wisdom you made them all; the earth is full of your creatures.* PSALM 104:24

> *There is the sea, vast and spacious, teeming with creatures beyond number — living things both large and small.* PSALM 104:25

They noticed.

Today try to very intentionally notice God's handiwork all around you. Ask God to open your eyes and help you see.

Day 11: Recovering Wonder

I wonder if distraction from God's voice in creation is not the most insidious of the many evils that our culture's clamor for amusement can bring. Because if I'm indoors staring at a screen all the time I'm missing something very important that God is saying:

> *Since the creation of the world God's invisible qualities — his eternal power and divine nature — have been clearly seen, being understood from what has been made, so that people are without excuse.* ROMANS 1:20

So notice His power and divine nature in what you see today. I'd also invite you to do something else: Notice the difference that *noticing* makes. How are you changed when you see evidence of His creative power?

And why not tell God about what you see that you find wondrous, just as you'd compliment a master artist?

God is... revealing Himself all around me.

QUESTIONS FOR REFLECTION:
What impresses you about Psalm 19?

Notice the difference that *noticing* God's power in the world around you makes to your attitude. How are you changed when you see evidence of His creative power?

What difference does it make to your attitude? To your stress level? To your sense of the powerful presence of God?

EYES WIDE OPEN

READ YOUR BIBLE: *Psalm 104:1–26*

SPOTLIGHT VERSE: *How many are your works, LORD! In wisdom you made them all; the earth is full of your creatures.* PSALM 104:24

MY WIFE AND I love snorkeling. One morning we read Psalm 104 together and got so excited about all its aquatic imagery that we said, "Let's go snorkeling right now and see all those *'teeming creatures beyond number—living things both large and small!'*" We agreed we'd see them all as reasons to worship, as examples of the Creator's art.

Twenty minutes later we were in the water, alone in an early morning ocean inlet... and were surprised to hear the faint sounds of dolphins!

Just listening to their "praise songs" was enough for me, but it got better: Their singing got louder and louder until a whole pod of them circled us, delighting us with their joyful leaps and dives.

They were above and below us, in front and in back of us, and on either side. They raced past, then returned to circle and splash and sing again.

To be honest, it was delightful and kind of scary all at the same time. What, I wondered, if they were *evil* dolphins? They could take us out like Flipper took out sharks every week!

But I only wondered that for about one second. Then the worry turned to worship.

All that would have been *fun* enough on any day, but what made it *transcendent* was the timing: We were framing everything we saw in terms of Psalm 104. Then to experience *this?*

We were both so moved spiritually that we were laughing and crying at the same time—and that's hard to do while wearing a snorkel! In fact, it's dangerous!

This was an exceptional experience—but little moments like this are all around you, all the time. Keeping your ears, eyes, and heart wide open for signs of God's power in creation is so important.

CURE FOR MY NEAR-SIGHTEDNESS

Seeing the thunderous wonders of God was a turning point for Job, who because of his terrible trials was asking the question, *"Why waste time trying to please God?"* (JOB 34:9 NLT).

But then God finally speaks to Job directly and draws his attention to the mysteries of creation in chapters 38–41.

Day 12: Eyes Wide Open

Read it to see an amazing sequence of descriptions of God's creative power.

It's interesting to me how in the first two chapters of this section, God starts big:

"Can you loosen Orion's belt?" JOB 38:31

and goes small:

"Do you watch when the doe bears her fawn?" JOB 39:1

and then zooms back out a little:

"Do you give the horse its strength or clothe its neck with a flowing mane?" JOB 39:19

as He points out that all around you, Job, everywhere you look, from constellation to gestation, from horses to hawks, there are mysteries to behold.

Job's response? He's drawn into awe and worship.

The God-rocket blasts off, and he's silenced into holy fear and reverence.

Someone told me once: "René, my biggest health problem is ingrown eyeballs." I think that's pretty much everyone's problem. It's a great description of what it's like to get caught in a loop of self-pitying or self-justifying or self-aggrandizing thoughts.

Got ingrown eyeballs? Get some wonder.

This might be one of the reasons I'm drawn to nature documentaries like *Planet Earth*. Particularly when seen

66

through the lens of what the Bible tells me about God, they both inspire me and put me in my place, like taking a ride through these chapters of the Book of Job!

God is... awesome in power.

QUESTIONS FOR REFLECTION:

Today look around you and journal about whatever strikes you as an example of God's creative power—especially if you've never noticed it before. *Intention* is a huge part of noticing God's omnipotence at work around you. Where today did you see evidence of the power of God?

If you have time, please read Job 38 and 39. Why do you think a meditation on creation was a big part of God's answer to Job?

How is this part of God's answer to your own questions and fears?

DAY 13
EX NIHILO

READ YOUR BIBLE: *Genesis 1:1–5*

SPOTLIGHT VERSE: *In the beginning God created the heavens and the earth.* GENESIS 1:1

HERE'S A MIND-BLOWER: GOD created everything that ever existed out of *absolutely nothing*. He didn't start with a blank canvas, or lump of clay, or a sheet of paper. There was zero for Him to work with.

Theologians have a Latin name for this: *ex nihilo*, which literally means *"out of nothing."* He creates something where there was nothing before, and He looks at it and says, *"It is good."*

This is a kind of creative power I have a hard time fathoming, because there isn't anything we humans make on our planet like that. You and I always start with previously existing materials in order to make something else.

Be sure to check out today's verses from Genesis 1.

Day 13: Ex Nihilo

The Hebrew word used there for *create* is *bara*. It's only used in the Old Testament when *God* creates.

When *human beings* create, there's another, lesser Hebrew word used. It's intended to express that, while our creativity reflects our creative God, we can't really produce *something out of nothing* the way God can.

Like Carl Sagan said, "If you wish to truly make an apple pie from scratch, you must first create the universe." [27]

Only God creates from scratch. But this is not just limited to the way God makes stars and planets. If you'll allow me to use *ex nihilo* poetically but truthfully, this is also related to how God *changes you*.

God is not held back by pre-existing conditions. He can do anything from scratch, bring anyone back to life again, when there are no resources, no hope, nothing.

Nihilo.

I think of the stories of some friends of mine…

About ten years ago, Kurtis was smoking pot for breakfast, lunch, and dinner. He didn't want to feel any pain; he didn't want to feel anything at all. His once well-muscled construction workers' body had been laid waste by multiple sclerosis. His marriage? Over. His career skills? Useless. He literally had nothing left. He was being warehoused in a nursing home for low-income patients, feeling no good to anyone. A big zero.

Nihilo.

Day 13: Ex Nihilo

One day Kurtis slipped out of the facility, steered his motorized wheelchair to the edge of a busy street, and tried to pick out a car that looked like the owner has good insurance—so he could roll into its path and end his suffering. But his nerve failed him and he rolled back to his room, feeling defeated even in his attempt at suicide—a new low, he thought.

Then a friend invited him to church. And from the first day Kurtis felt something stirring—something alive, happy, playful, all around him. He tells me he now believes it was the Holy Spirit breathing new life into his dead soul. The Spirit moved across what was formless and void.

To see Kurtis now, worshipping with tears flowing, leading the residents' advocacy group at the nursing center, or greeting people at church with the biggest grin in the building, you wouldn't recognize him. His wheelchair is plastered with signs he prints out from his computer ("He Is Risen Indeed!" says one). He is in many ways brand-new.

Then there's my friend Robert. He went into the family business several years ago: Importing and exporting… drugs. With no trace of conscience, he happily funneled millions of dollars of drugs, mostly cocaine, into the U.S. It was a booming market. Until he got busted and sent to prison. And his marriage crumbled. And his daughter was murdered. And he lost everything. He was left with *nothing*.

Nihilo.

But then, spiritual truths Robert had first heard as a child began to finally take effect as he attended prison Bible studies. A faith muscle started to grow where there had been nothing before.

Fast-forward to the present-day. The man I know smiles more than almost anyone else at church, unless he is weeping with brokenness when thinking of the addicts he helped create.

His occupation? He's a counselor. His specialty? Addictions. Helping others get off the path he once trod. God looked at his total darkness and said, *"Let there be light."* And Robert *shines*.

"Omnipotence": It's not just a fancy theological term. It means God sees possibilities where no one else sees them.

It means there is always hope.

It means God delights in His creative skill every time He produces a masterpiece out of a life seemingly devoid of hope or promise.

And it means He steps back and looks at His work in *you* and says, *"It is good."*

You've been keeping your eyes wide open for signs of His finesse in nature—now watch for signs of His power in changed lives all around you.

And the next time you see someone and think, "there is no hope there—nothing," remember how God likes to work:

Ex nihilo.

God is… not limited by anything.

Day 13: Ex Nihilo

QUESTIONS FOR REFLECTION:

What does it mean that God creates *ex nihilo?*

How could this truth inspire and motivate you in your daily life, and as you look at the challenges and the needy people around you?

DAY 14
INFINITE POWER,
INFINITE POSSIBILITIES

READ YOUR BIBLE: *Ephesians 1:18–23*

SPOTLIGHT VERSE: *Now to him who is able to do immea-surably more than all we ask or imagine, according to his power that is at work within us, to him be glory in the church and in Christ Jesus throughout all genera-tions, for ever and ever! Amen.* EPHESIANS 3:20–21

MEDITATING ON THE POWER of God is important.

One of the many times the opponents of Jesus tried to lure him into a debate, Christ's response was this:

> *"You are in error because you do not know the Scriptures or the power of God."* MATTHEW 22:29

I wonder how many times I am in error because of the same thing?

Day 14: Infinite Power, Infinite Possibilities

When I worry that all my efforts as a pastor are weak and ineffective...

When I lose hope about a friend who is blowing it...

When I wonder if I'll ever conquer that habit...

When I worry about my future...

When I worry about my kids...

I am in error because I do not know the *Scriptures* or *the power of God.*

MORE THAN POSITIVE THINKING

When times get tough, I find that the tough usually get stuck in the old stand-by: Positive thinking.

Generally speaking I'm happy to try to be a positive thinker. After all, that's better than being a negative thinker. But what do you do when the negative circumstances overwhelm you?

The way through is to realize that you are helpless. *Powerless.*

But then you realize what *Scripture* says about the *power of God.*

> *I am the* LORD, *the God of all mankind; is anything too difficult for me?* JEREMIAH 32:27

> *Nothing is impossible for God.* LUKE 1:37

> *I pray that you will be able to understand the incredible greatness of His power for us who believe*

74

Day 14: Infinite Power, Infinite Possibilities

Him. This is the same mighty power that raised Christ from the dead. EPHESIANS 1:19–20A (NLT)

GOD'S POWER IN YOU

Think of all the ways we've meditated on God's power together this week. Now realize that same God wants to use that power *in you*.

As Paul says in today's spotlight verses:

"Now to Him who is able to do…" God is able. Worried about whether you'll ever overcome that habit? Concerned you're not equipped to raise children? Anxious about making ends meet? God is able. Able to help. Able to empower. Able to do…

"More… than we can ask." Now, I can ask for a lot. But God can do more. And He can do…

"More than we can… imagine." I have a pretty good imagination! But He can do more. In fact, He can do…

"Immeasurably more than all we can ask or imagine."

What do you ask God for—or perhaps just imagine, without daring to even ask?

To find a spouse?

To have a child?

To write a book?

To be healed?

To find peace as you enter old age?

To control your urges?

To heal your marriage?

Why do we think this stuff is too hard for God? I'm not saying He'll answer all these prayers the way you want them answered—because, what's the verse say? He is able to do *more than* we ask or imagine. His answer is, ultimately, more—immeasurably more, better, richer—than what we had imagined.

Are you ready for that adventure?

God is... able.

QUESTIONS FOR REFLECTION:
Although you may theoretically believe that God is omnipotent, does your life demonstrate your belief?

Why do you think you—or other believers—may not be experiencing the power of God as frequently as He seems to wish to provide it?

How might your life change if you truly internalized the truth of God's omnipotence?

What powerful things do you expect God to do in your life?

WEEK 3

GOD IS

Omnipresent

The central promise in the Bible is not "I will forgive you," although of course that promise is there. The most frequent promise in the Bible is "I will be with you." JOHN ORTBERG

DAY 15

NO LONGER ALONE

READ YOUR BIBLE: *Psalm 46*

SPOTLIGHT VERSE: *God is our refuge and strength, an ever-present help in trouble.* PSALM 46:1

ONE OF THE LAST things Elvis Presley ever wrote was a note he crumpled up and threw away. According to *USA Today*, an aide saw him toss it into a trash can and fished it out the morning Elvis was found dead. It read in part:

"I feel so *alone* sometimes. Help me, Lord." [28]

Alfred Hitchcock, the most famous film director of his day, spoke these mysterious words on his deathbed:

"I am lost in… a sea of… *alone*." [29]

Albert Einstein, the most recognizable face of the 20th century, said:

"It is strange to be known so universally and yet to be so *alone*." [30]

Day 15: No Longer Alone

My guess is that you can relate.

Tom Wolfe, author of *Bonfire of the Vanities*, said "Loneliness is the most common human experience." [31]

Mother Teresa observed, "Loneliness is the poverty of the Western world." [32]

LONELY PLANET

And it seems to be getting worse. Despite the popularity of social media, a Carnegie-Mellon research project showed that the more time people spend online, the lonelier they perceive themselves to be. [33]

This is serious.

Dr. James Lynch is the author of another study showing lonely adults have a death rate twice as high as adults who are not lonely. Loneliness, he says, is a "lethal poison." [34]

What's the cure for this epidemic of loneliness?

While human companionship is essential, I believe deep down we're longing for connection to the One who will never leave us. Our thirst is filled only by the God who is *here*, the God who always was here and always will be here.

Theologians call this the *omnipresence* of God.

HE IS WITH YOU

Omnipresence means all-present. God is everywhere. To be more precise, God is in every place, all the time.

He's right there when you're hurting.

Day 15: No Longer Alone

He's right there when you're tempted.

He's right there when you feel weak.

Omnipresence does *not* mean God is every thing. That's *pantheism*. That equates the Creator with the creation.

According to the Bible, everything is not God, although God is everywhere and created everything. He exists independently of His creation, like an artist and his painting. If nothing in creation existed, there would still be God, who alone is uncreated.

This may be the most difficult attribute of God for humans to understand because we live in a three-dimensional world—we're limited by space and time. So usually when we think of *omnipresence* we think it means something like this: God is so big that a layer of God is spread out over all of creation, like a blanket— as if there's a part of God in Santa Cruz, a part of God down in Brazil, and a part of Him way past Jupiter. But that wouldn't be *omnipresence*; that would just be *immensity*.

This is an important distinction, because most of us were raised with a sense of God's *transcendence*—which is true. God is transcendent, higher, *beyond*. But *omnipresence* teaches God is also *always intensely near*.

Omnipresence means *all* of God is *everywhere at once*. God is free from the constraints of time and space, so all of Him can be everywhere at the same time.

Day 15: No Longer Alone

PRESENT AND PRESENT-TENSE

To say that God is omnipresent means this statement is always true:

"All of God is right here, right now."

100% of God is here with me now as I write these words.

100% of God is there with you as you read these words.

And even though I wrote these words before you read these words, God is with us both simultaneously!

Psalm 46 emphasizes this: It opens by saying God is *ever-present*.

Different commentators have tried to capture the intent of this Hebrew phrase in words like: He is always immediately present; He never withdraws; He is close at our side and ready to help.

Psalm 46 goes on to twice repeat that *He is with us*. Because he believes this, the author says, he will never fear—*"even if the earth gives way!"* And we know something about the fear that can grip you during an earthquake or landslide here in California!

WHY DO I FEEL A DISTANCE?

Most people think of God not as very present, but as very remote. I think that's because we have an accurate a sense of our distance from God's *holiness*—while God is everywhere, we are metaphorically a million miles away from God's righteousness.

This is the feeling of *spiritual alienation* the Bible talks about.

When Psalmists write that they long for God's closeness, or that it feels like God has abandoned them, they don't mean that God's presence is actually removed. That's impossible. They mean that they sense a distance from Him, that they are alienated from His holy nature because of their sin.

THE BIBLE IS ABOUT CLOSENESS

The Bible is nothing less than the story of how God bridges the spiritual gap between Him and us.

Within the Trinity, The Father, Son, and Holy Spirit, the three persons in one God, enjoy close fellowship forever. Then when God's creation rebels against Him and runs away, the Trinity has a rescue plan:

The Father reveals His presence to us through creation.

But He does much more: He sends the Son.

In Jesus Christ, God not only came to be near to us for a human lifetime; He died on the cross so that the alienation between you and God can be ended forever.

When the veil in the Jerusalem temple separating the Holy of Holies from the rest of the world was miraculously torn in two at the death of Christ, it showed what God had accomplished. Your sins can be forgiven and you can live in God's closeness.

Then the Son asks the Father to send the Holy Spirit so that you have God's guiding presence always: *"I will ask the*

Day 15: No Longer Alone

Father, and he will give you another Counselor to be with you forever." (JOHN 14:16)

In fact, read John 14–17, Jesus' last message to the disciples before his crucifixion, and notice how much He talks about closeness and friendship. *Intimacy with you is high on God's agenda*; it's important to Him that you know about his plan to make His presence manifest to you.

And then one day all alienation between humanity and God will end, as heaven and earth are made one.

The whole Bible is the story of God drawing nearer to you and me, bridging the alienation you and I sense. And if God went to all that effort, it's safe to say He wants you to *know* how His close He is to you *right now!*

This week let's explore some of the amazing, life-changing implications of God's omnipresence. I pray that God's presence is made manifest to you as you study!

God is… here.

QUESTIONS FOR REFLECTION:

Try to summarize, in one short sentence, what the omnipresence of God means to you:

When you don't focus on God's omnipresence, what negative or destructive thoughts or emotions do you struggle with?

In Psalm 46, what difference does the psalmist say God's presence makes on his emotions and attitudes?

PRACTICING HIS PRESENCE

READ YOUR BIBLE: *Psalm 16:8–11*

SPOTLIGHT VERSE: *Blessed are those who have learned to acclaim you, who walk in the light of your presence, O LORD.* PSALM 89:15

YOU MIGHT BE THINKING, "The omnipresence of God may be true in theory, but why don't I *feel* God's presence all the time?"

Well, it may be that you are sensing a spiritual alienation because of your sin. God longs to bridge that distance. You can simply receive His free, lavish, gracious gift of reconciliation through Christ.

But could there be other reasons you're not aware of God's presence?

Some of the time I think God hides His presence from my *feelings* to develop my *faith* muscle. When I can't see or feel Him, I need to have faith that He is there.

Day 16: Practicing His Presence

But much of time, I think God is *longing* for me to sense His presence. It's just that I'm out of practice.

THE SOLDIER MONK

Nicholas Herman was born around 1610 in France. He was a professional soldier, fighting in the Thirty Years War, where he was nearly killed and his sciatic nerve was severely injured. He was left disabled and in chronic pain for the rest of his life.

But after the war he decided to enter a monastery, changing his name to Brother Lawrence.

He had great visions of being an intellectual monk, or a Bible-copying monk, but was instead assigned to be the new monastery's cook. A cook-monk. And then, after fifteen years, they promoted him to be… the sandal repair man. Initially he felt disappointed and insignificant, but it was while he performed these daily chores over those many years that he learned how to develop an awareness of God's presence.

Another monk interviewed him and wrote a brilliant little book based on those conversations that is still a bestseller hundreds of years later: *The Practice of the Presence of God*. It's long been in the public domain, so you can download a complete copy for free. It's fascinating to me that the monk who was, technically, lowest on the ladder is the only one still remembered from that monastery to this day!

One of the things I love about Brother Lawrence is that he is very self-deprecating, and talks bluntly about how the "discipline" of daily devotions never worked for him: "He could never regulate his devotion by certain methods as

85

some do. At first, he had practiced meditation but, after some time, that went off…"

Yet he meditated on God informally all the time. Here's some of his advice:

> We should feed and nourish our soul with high notions of God… [and] we should establish ourselves in a sense of God's presence by continually conversing with Him… we ought to act with God in the greatest simplicity, speaking to Him frankly and plainly, and imploring His assistance in our affairs just as they happen. [35]

In these constant, almost casual conversations, Brother Lawrence had a sense of the nearness of God that has inspired millions of readers in the centuries since his book was first written.

That is something of what it means to *"walk in the light of God's presence,"* to *"learn to acclaim Him."*

THERE'S PRESENCE AND THERE'S PRESENCE

When I was younger I was very judgmental of Christian songs and hymns that expressed a desire to be "in God's presence." I loved to correct people, "Don't you know you are *always* in God's presence?"

Now I understand what those songs are talking about: You could differentiate between God's *metaphysical* presence and God's *manifest* presence.

His *metaphysical* presence means He is essentially always with me. Nothing can ever change that. His *manifest* presence is what those songs are about. The Bible says God's metaphysical presence is everywhere, even in the very depths of hell. But, as A.W. Tozer put it, "It is the manifest, conscious presence of God that makes heaven heaven." [36]

Expressing a longing to be in the presence of God is really a request that God give you the blessing of *awareness* of His presence.

TUNING IN TO GOD

Like Brother Lawrence learned, you can discover this in every minor, even mundane, moment of your day.

He practiced an awareness of the presence of God in the monastery kitchen and cobbler's shop, two places that for the monks were places of drudgery, as far removed from the meditative environment of their chapel as they could imagine.

Maybe for you, time spent in your car commuting to work, or from errand to errand, feels something like that. So imagine trying his method on the freeway:

See the leaves on the trees just over the sound wall? The sunlight is showing through them so they seem to be glowing. Just as God shines through His creation. Think of the complicated DNA woven by God even into these common things.

The birds on the power lines? God's spectacular design of these creatures to enable them to fly is amazing.

The clouds overhead? The water vapor they contain is among the most precious substances in the universe.

Notice the people in the cars next to you? God loves them so much that He died for them.

Hear the joy expressed in the music you are listening to? The Bible says music is part of the fabric of creation; the angels sang before there was even an earth, so music is truly a deep, mysterious way to join with all that God made to sing to His glory.

Now see it all at once. Perceive it as a reminder that it's all a gift, that God did not need to make any of this, but He did, and that the same God who made it all longs to know you, and is all around you revealing His glories even now.

It struck me one day that the sense of God's manifest presence, that blend of serenity and joy and peace and purpose and love that flows into and out of you in those moments, is the exact opposite of feeling guilt and shame. Like the Bible says:

> *In Your presence is fullness of joy;*
> *At Your right hand are pleasures forevermore.*
> PSALM 16:11B (NKJV)

What a gift from God!

But you can do your part. You can develop the habit of affirming that, wherever you are…

God is… here now.

Day 16: Practicing His Presence

QUESTIONS FOR REFLECTION:

What are some helpful ways you have found to "practice the presence of God"?

In what area of your life do you need to focus on practicing the presence of God? How could this make a difference in your life?

NO SOLO FLIGHTS

READ YOUR BIBLE: *Psalm 139:7–17*

SPOTLIGHT VERSE: *Where can I go from your Spirit? Where can I flee from your presence?* PSALM 139:7

IMPOSSIBLY GREEN BANANA TREE leaves, deep red tropical flowers, and the dense, vine-like branches of a banyan tree frame the narrow road as my wife and I drive to the nearly hidden grave of Charles Lindbergh.

In his life Lindbergh had traveled all over the globe, achieving rock-star like fame in an era before rock stars. Millions admired him for making the first solo nonstop airplane flight across the Atlantic in May 1927.

Yet he spent his last few winters in the tiny town of Kipahulu on the jungle-like east coast of Maui, Hawaii, far from the throngs of fans that greeted him everywhere else.

His only public appearances? Every Sunday, he and his wife went to the tiny local church.

Day 17: No Solo Flights

In mid-August, 1974, Lindbergh was told by doctors back in New York that his cancer-ravaged body was near death. They urged him to stay there in the hospital, but he told them, "I would rather live one day in Maui than one month in New York."

So back to Maui he went, where he immediately began sketching precise designs for his grave. He decided it would not include a word about any of his achievements.

Only his name. And Psalm 139:9 — *"If I take the wings of the morning, and dwell in the uttermost parts of the sea…"*

Lindbergh died just days after his arrival back in Maui, and his gravestone was engraved precisely as he designed.

As Laurie and I stand at the grave and drop a hibiscus flower onto Lindbergh's headstone, I wonder if he left just that one verse on his headstone as an invitation for curious visitors to find out for themselves how the quote ends.

Because the next words from Psalm 139 are:

> *…even there your hand will guide me, your right hand will hold me fast.*

King David, the author of the Psalm 139, seems stunned by this realization.

This was a totally new idea for religions of David's era, about 1000 B.C. People then thought of their gods as limited by space and time: There was the god of the sky, the god of the sea, the god of the underworld. They had bodies, and they could only be in one place at a time.

But through divine revelation David understands this is not true of God. He is the God of *all* those places, and *all* of God is *always* in *all* of them.

THERE WHEN YOU WERE FORMED

Maybe the hardest verses for you to believe for yourself are the ones about God's presence with David even in his mother's womb.

> *You made all the delicate, inner parts of my body and knit me together in my mother's womb. Thank you for making me so wonderfully complex! Your work-manship is marvelous — how well I know it.*
> PSALM 139:13–14 (NLT)

Christian counselor David Seamands writes about a woman named Betty. Her parents felt forced to wed because her mother was pregnant with her. It was an undesired marriage and Betty was an undesired child. When Betty was three and a half, her father left.

She carried the sense of being an unwanted accident with her for her entire life. Then one day at the end of a counseling session Dr. Seamands gave her some homework.

He said, "I want you to imagine the very moment of your conception, the instant that cell from your mother was fertilized by that cell from your father. As you think about that, ask yourself one question: *Where was God at that moment?*"

When they met a week later, Betty told him that at first she thought the whole assignment was crazy. But about the third day, when she really began concentrating on it, she began to cry. And she wrote down this prayer in her journal:

> O God, my heart leaps with the thought that you, my loving father, have never forsaken me. You were there when I was conceived in earthly lust. You looked upon me with a father's love even then. You were thinking of me in my mother's womb, molding me...
>
> You were there when my mother gave birth to me, standing in the vacant place of my father. You were there when I cried the bitter tears of a child whose father has abandoned her. You were holding me in your gentle arms all the while, rocking me gently in your soothing love.
>
> Oh, why did I not know of your presence? God, my dear, dear Father, my heart had turned to frost, but the light of your love is beginning to warm it. [37]

God's *metaphysical* presence was made *manifest* presence for her in retrospect, as the Holy Spirit helped her think back on that time in her life.

It goes for you too.

Anything you went through in your life? God was there.

Anything you're going through now? He's there too.

Anything you will go through? God will be there.

Omnipresence means God was with you in your past, and it means He will be with you in the future.

Day 17: No Solo Flights

After his solo flight across the Atlantic Ocean, reporters asked Lindbergh how he handled that all alone. He answered, "*Is* he alone who has courage on his right hand and faith on his left hand?" [38]

While he left no explanation for his gravestone, I imagine that while Lindbergh was preparing for his final great solo flight, he was reminding himself of that very truth, thinking something like: "It's ok. God was with me on those flights, God is with me now, God will go through my final journey with me, and God will be waiting for me on the other side."

My own father experienced this. When he was dying of cancer, his last words were:

"It's like a dream… God is all around me."

And then he died.

Lindbergh. My dad. They learned: You *never* really fly solo.

As you go through your day today, remind yourself:

God is… with me, and will be with me, always.

QUESTIONS FOR REFLECTION:

What intrigues or impacts you about Psalm 139:7–17?

These verses speak of God's presence in various places and times in life. Which of these images has the most impact to you right now? Why?

How could it change someone's attitudes and emotions to really believe God will be present with them through death?

THE LORD IS IN THIS PLACE

READ YOUR BIBLE: *Hebrews 13:5–6*

SPOTLIGHT VERSE: *Be strong and courageous. Do not be afraid or terrified because of them, for the* LORD *your God goes with you; he will never leave you nor forsake you.* DEUTERONOMY 31:6

ONE DAY WHEN I was in grade school my mother found me crumpled in the hallway crying. The next day was "Bring Dad To School Day"—and I didn't have anyone to bring.

As I mentioned yesterday, my dad died of cancer. That happened a month before my 4th birthday. Loneliness, and I mean *bone-deep* loneliness, soon set in, lasting for years, and resulting in many scenes like the one in the hallway that day.

I will never forget what happened next.

My mom, who had not been a Christian for very long, sat down on the floor next to me, hugged me, and spoke words of deep theology:

You know, René, most kids don't have what you have. You have not one, but *two* fathers in heaven! And while your dad Fred can't be with you anymore, your Heavenly Father is always with you.

He is with you every time you walk to school,
and every time you are on the playground,
and every time you play a sport,
and every time you eat lunch,
take a test,
walk home...
He will *never* leave you.

She was explaining one practical result of believing in the *omnipresence* of God: He is not just there as an omnipresent *Watcher*—He is a *participant*. He is my Savior. My Comforter. My ever-present Helper in times of trouble.

YOUR PAST AND YOUR FUTURE

Maybe, like me, you experienced the loss of a parent through death. Or there was a different loss, through divorce or separation.

Maybe you moved so much while growing up that you never had a chance to make lasting friends. You were always the new kid.

Maybe you've always felt like the odd person out in school, at work, and even in your family. You've been left more times than you care to recount.

And now, when meeting new people, you're crippled by a sense of suspicion and inevitability. You wonder who is going to hurt you this time. You look at the future and see not a promised land of new friends and relationships but just the likelihood of more broken dreams.

In Deuteronomy 31, the people of Israel are on the edge of the Promised Land. After 40 hard years on the move in the desert, they're terrified. Moses is dying, they've got a new leader, everything's changing, they're afraid of their future, and they're afraid of their enemies. Then Moses raises his hands and as part of his final pep talk says:

> *Do not be afraid or terrified because of them, for the* L ORD *your God goes with you; he will never leave you nor forsake you.* DEUTERONOMY 31:6

He will *never* leave you or forsake you.

Nothing and no one else can say that.

To the people of Israel God is saying, *"Even when Moses dies, I'll still be right here. I will **never** leave you."*

And God is saying the same thing to you.

Even if your leader dies

Even if your family leaves you

Even if your spouse abandons you

Even if your children reject you

I will never, ever leave you nor forsake you.

Ever.

Day 18: The Lord is in This Place

CONTENTMENT AND OMNIPRESENCE

In today's reading in Hebrews, the writer quotes that verse from Deuteronomy, and his application is this: Keep your life free from the love of money and a desire for stuff you don't have. Because *God will never leave you nor forsake you.*

How is *contentment* related to the omnipresence of God?

Well, when you have abandonment issues, it can be easy to find comfort in your *stuff*. It makes you feel like you've arrived in some sense, and it can be an attempt to show those who've judged you that you've made it—or an attempt to gain their approval.

But if you know that God is with you, the need for that fades.

THE LORD IS IN THIS PLACE

Writing on the omnipresence of God, Bill Hybels suggests a phrase to say out loud when afraid or lonely: *"The Lord is in this place."*

That phrase comes from the story of Jacob in the Bible. He sees a vision of God and says, *"Surely the Lord was in this place, and I knew it not!"* (GENESIS 28:16)

That was his trouble. And that's our trouble. The Lord is always here, but we know it not.

Tempted? Say it. Scared? Lonely? Intimidated? Overwhelmed? Try repeating that phrase until its truth comforts you...

Day 18: The Lord is in This Place

"The Lord is in this place."

"The *Lord* is in this place."

"The Lord is in *this* place."

QUESTIONS FOR REFLECTION:

In what areas of life do you need to be *"strong and courageous"* right now?

How can an awareness of God's presence make the difference?

HE'S THERE IN THE DARKNESS

READ YOUR BIBLE: *Psalm 23:1–4*

SPOTLIGHT VERSE: *Even though I walk through the darkest valley, I will fear no evil, for you are with me; your rod and your staff, they comfort me.* PSALM 23:4

ONE OF THE MOST profound letters I've received recently was from a man who heard me speak at a summer conference:

> I first heard you speak a couple years ago. At the time it had been 9 years since my son had died (at 4 months old) of a genetic disease. For 4 months, I asked one question: Why my son?
>
> After the funeral I stood there like so many have done before me and yelled at God: Why my son? Why? Why? Why? My God, who saved my soul and loved me, tell me the %$&!ing reason!!!

I was so mad, and so focused on wanting things in my own control, that I stood there for a long time, defiant, thinking "I will not give one inch until I get an answer!" But I didn't get an answer.

Right after this, I went downhill. I went into depression, lost my job, took medication to keep me sane. My wife and other son stood there wondering why I had flipped out and couldn't accept what happened.

"Come on, Daddy, you know Brady's in heaven," my 3-year-old son would say! "You know that Jesus and His Dad are taking care of him!" A 3-year-old would say this, but a grown adult wouldn't accept it.

As you can imagine, life was not too good at home. There were constant battles.

Well I have to tell you, the service that night two years ago touched not only my mind, but my soul deep inside. I felt like my whole soul was being exposed and opened up. All the rotting stench that I had carried with me and even worshipped was all in front of me. Nine years of standing there, gritting my teeth and growling at God—how could I have even heard Him if He *was* talking to me?

Later at communion I sat in the back pew with my wife waiting for the service to get over with… I bowed my head… and all of a sudden it was like everything changed around me. I don't know if you can understand, but it was like everything else disappeared and I was sitting in the pew all by myself with no one there. I sat there crying with my head down and then had a sense of the warm Spirit of God touching me.

Then it was as if God's Spirit whispered to me, "It's ok, it's ok... he is with me... I will take care of him, and he will be very well taken care of, so don't worry. And I am always here for you, too. So don't worry."

I sat there and cried—like my whole being was being transformed and healed with this warmth throughout my body and soul.

The next thing I knew, I was aware of being in the communion service again, with all the noise and the people around me. I went up and took communion, and for the first time in nine years understood again what communion was about.

Now, to the depths of my being, I understood the answer to my question.

Jesus did come and die for us, but more than just dying like my son, he was raised again and is living in heaven by his Father, while He is also sitting next to me all the time, loving me, and while He is loving me, he is loving my son Brady too!

I understand that no matter what, God's love for me is *always there*, even when I stood for nine years rejecting it. He loves me.

Well, now every time I take communion I cry a little bit. I cry because of what I know is so very true! My life has passion again!

Even though you walk through the darkest valley, He is right there with you.

The Lord does not always lead you *around* the valley of the shadow of death, But when you are *in* it, He is right there, leading you all the way through to green pastures, quiet waters, and His house, where you will dwell forever.

God is... with me in my darkest times.

QUESTIONS FOR REFLECTION:

How does this man's letter impact you?

Name all of the benefits of God's presence listed in Psalm 23.

HE'S THERE IN DEEP WATERS

READ YOUR BIBLE: *Isaiah 43:1–5.*

SPOTLIGHT VERSE: *When you go through deep waters, I will be with you. When you go through rivers of difficulty, you will not drown.* ISAIAH 43:2A (NLT)

DEEP WATERS. WHEN I read those words in today's Bible verse, I think of my friend Phil's sister Kathy.

She was on a sailboat off the coast of Santa Cruz Island near Santa Barbara, California, when huge swells capsized the boat and knocked her into the water.

She was lost at sea. Clinging to one small square seat cushion.

The U.S. Coast Guard sent a ship and a helicopter to look for her. She could see the helicopter circling above, but the crew couldn't see her.

An hour went by. Then six, seven, eight hours. And finally, at midnight, the search for Kathy was called off. They phoned her brother, my friend Phil. He still calls it "The night Kathy died." The caller told him, "No one can survive in these waters for this long. We are now looking for a body, not a survivor."

When I talked to Kathy about what happened next, she began to cry as she remembered, "The presence of God was so real to me — it was like God was right there with me."

Kathy told me, "I almost felt cheated when I was rescued. I was praying, singing hymns… first I panicked, but then the peace of God took over."

IN THE DEEP
Notice in today's reading, God never says you won't go through deep water and great troubles.

What's the promise?

When you do, I will be with you.

Maybe you're going through deep rivers right now. You can relate to Kathy: You feel like you're treading water, your feet can't touch bottom, all you can see all around you is the deep blue sea. None of us can predict the problems we'll face in life, or how they'll end. But of this you can be certain: God's going through it with you.

GOD IS WHERE?
Josh McDowell put a long word on the screen during one of his lectures. I was puzzled as I read it:

Day 20: He's There in Deep Waters

GODISNOWHERE.

Josh let us try to figure it out for a minute. Then he asked, "What does that say?" Most people answered, *"God is nowhere."* But as Josh pointed out, you can just as easily read, *"God is now here."* [39]

It's all about keeping those eyes wide open. When you pray and it seems like nothing is happening, you might be tempted to conclude, "God is nowhere."

But that's not when God *leaves*. That's when God *takes over*. So relax, knowing you're always in the palm of His hand.

How was Kathy rescued?

When the Coast Guard called off the search and turned to go back to port, they literally bumped right into her. The bow of the ship almost ran her over, and she slapped weakly on the hull as the ship went past. A crew member thought he heard something and yelled for a full stop.

When they finally hoisted her on board, they asked, "Who are you?"

She said, "Well, I guess I'm the one you've been looking for!"

And Kathy tells me one crew member then exclaimed, "Wow! I've never actually found anyone before!"

THE GOD OF CLOSENESS

Kathy's rescue seems miraculous. But she told me, "René, the greatest miracle of the night by far was God's amazing closeness to me."

Day 20: He's There in Deep Waters

When you pass through the waters,
I will be with you...

What I love about today's passage is that it contains so many awe-inspiring attributes of God that we've looked at already in this study: It reminds me that He's Holy, the Lord, the Creator... yet the predominant promise is about His *closeness*. He wants me to hear, "Fear not... you are mine... I have redeemed you... I will be with you."

You could say He is *the God of eternal intimacy.*

ETERNAL INTIMACY

You see this in the Trinity.

See, God is all about relationship, closeness, intimacy, love. But could those attributes simply go unexpressed for inconceivable stretches of time before anything was created? If there was a time when He had no one to love or be close to, then how can we say His presence and intimacy and love are eternal attributes?

That is why, to me, it makes sense that there is the Trinity. One God, three Persons. So that even before anything else existed, the attributes of God were always being expressed perfectly within the godhead. There was relationship, intimacy, love, omniscience, presence, all right there, in ages past.

And you see the Trinity in the plan of redemption.

Day 20: He's There in Deep Waters

INTENSIFYING INTIMACY

The Father's plans from before creation are all about diminishing the distance between us and God. He reveals Himself in creation and through Scripture...

Then the Son comes to Earth and walks among us and dies for us so that the alienation between man and God would end....

Then the Holy Spirit is sent to walk with and within us every moment, guiding, teaching, sanctifying...

And the Father's plans are fulfilled when one day heaven and earth are one, the dwelling of God is with men, and there is no longer even need for a temple because *God is with us.*

The intimacy keeps intensifying.

It all means that there is hope for the future. And help for the present.

No matter what mess you find yourself in, whether it's your fault or not, whether others are aware of it or not...

God is... with me and within me.

QUESTIONS FOR REFLECTION:

What is promised in Isaiah 43:1–5?

What is **not** promised?

What "waters, rivers, fires," as Isaiah 43:1–5 puts it, have you gone through during which an awareness of God's presence made a difference for you?

What "waters, rivers, fires" are you passing through now?

Thank God for His presence there with you, right now. Throughout the day, remind yourself again: "The Lord is in this place!"

HE'S THERE THROUGH IT ALL

READ YOUR BIBLE: *Joshua 1:7–9*

SPOTLIGHT VERSE: *"Have I not commanded you? Be strong and courageous. Do not be afraid; do not be discouraged, for the LORD your God will be with you wherever you go."* JOSHUA 1:9

THE AMAZING STORY OF explorer Sir Ernest Shackleton and his famous ship *Endurance* has been the subject of a best-selling book and an award-winning film.

During his voyage to the South Pole, ice trapped and crushed his ship. Shackleton and three of his sailors left the rest of the crew and made their way in an open lifeboat over 800 miles of stormy Atlantic sea.

They then crawled over slippery glaciers and forbidding mountain peaks until they finally reached a manned outpost—and then the next day they turned around and went back to rescue every single person who stayed behind near the shipwreck.

Day 21: He's There Through It All

That journey through hundreds of miles of the most alien landscape on earth is still a stunner. But how did he do it? Neither the book nor the movie will tell you what Shackleton himself said was key.

After his return to London, Shackleton revealed where he found the strength for his amazing trip. He said in a speech, referring to the biblical story of Shadrach, Meshach, and Abednego in Daniel 3:

> We all felt that there were not three, but four of us. When I look back upon those days, with all their anxiety and peril, I cannot doubt that our party was divinely guided... afterwards Worsley said to me, "Boss, I had a curious feeling that there was another person with us." I can honestly say that it wasn't bad. We always felt that there was something above... you all know the words, "If I take the wings of the morning and dwell in the uttermost parts of the sea, even there shall thy hand lead me..." That 139th Psalm exactly fitted our case. [40]

He knew the ever-present help of God.

YOU CAN REST SECURE

Before his death, Moses pronounces blessings on each of the twelve tribes of Israel, and he says something beautiful about Benjamin that is true of every believer:

> *Let the beloved of the LORD rest secure in him, for he shields him all day long, and the one the LORD loves rests between his shoulders.* DEUTERONOMY 33:12

I think of a small child asleep even while riding on Daddy's shoulders, his drowsy head resting on his father's head. Or a little helpless lamb carried on the broad back of a kind shepherd. Like them, you rest *"between His shoulders."*

When Shackleton left on his last adventure, years after his amazing rescue of the *Endurance* crew, he knew he would probably not return alive. Intriguingly, he insisted on taking with him a primitive recording of a woman singing the hymn, *Abide With Me*. Some of the lyrics:

> "I need thy presence every passing hour;
> In life, in death, O Lord, abide with me!"

He listened to that record as he died, apparently confident that the God who had been with him through the icy waters near the South Pole would lead him through the valley of the shadow of death.

God is... with me through the valley of the shadow of death.

QUESTIONS FOR REFLECTION:

Read Deuteronomy 33:12 out loud. Have you ever thought of yourself as "resting between the shoulders" of a loving God? What do you think this image is intended to convey?

Particularly if you've been feeling anxious and abandoned, what steps can you take to practically change your thinking to reflect the truth that the "Fourth Man" is with you? (More on that tomorrow!)

WEEK 4

GOD IS

Love

If once we accept it as true that the whole Power behind this astonishing Universe is of that kind of character that Christ could only describe as "Father", the whole of life is transfigured. J. B. PHILLIPS

HOW GOD DESCRIBES HIMSELF

READ YOUR BIBLE: *Exodus 34:1–10*

SPOTLIGHT VERSE: *The LORD, the LORD, the compassionate and gracious God, slow to anger, abounding in love and faithfulness.* EXODUS 34:6

THIS IS A STUDY about knowing God better.

When you want to know what someone's like, you could ask other people who know that person.

Or you could go right to the source: You could meet the person you're interested in, hang out, ask questions.

That's exactly what Moses does. With God.

In Exodus 33:18. Moses says, *"I beg you, show me your glory!"*

And God answers.

Day 22: How God Describes Himself

Now, after all the wonders God showed Job, after all the creative masterpieces you saw the Psalmists singing about, after the omnipresence we studied last week, what would you expect God to reveal? What kind of scorching, lightning-bolt flash of shock and awe comes next?

What, specifically, is His *glory?*

What comes next is God's great self-description. It's the moment God defines Himself, God's answer to the question, "What are you like?"

I mean, this is huge.

God is telling me what He wants me to really, really make sure I know about Him.

My suspicion that this is of major importance is confirmed by theologian J. Carl Laney. He points out how many times God's words in these verses are quoted in the Old Testament. Ready for the list? These words are reiterated in Numbers 14:18; Nehemiah 9:17; Psalm 103:8,17; 145:8; Jeremiah 32:18–19; Joel 2:13; and Jonah 4:2. [41] Whew.

And that doesn't even count how many times *paraphrases* of these words are in the Bible. Since you ask: They're in Deuteronomy 5:9–10; 1 Kings 3:6; Lamentations 3:32; Daniel 9:4; and Nahum 1:3.

So the writers of the Bible obviously thought this was pretty important, a foundational statement about what God is like.

But here's something strange: As Laney points out, modern theologians hardly mention these verses when discussing God's attributes. In fact, in the massive classic *Systematic*

Theology by L. S. Chafer, he doesn't even quote these verses at all, in hundreds of pages describing God! Somehow this has fallen off the radar.

Yet this is how God describes Himself.

I think we'd better take a closer look.

The historical context is crucial: This comes at a moral low point for Israel.

In Exodus 32, Moses is meeting with God on Mount Sinai to get the tablets of the law. Meanwhile, the people of Israel decide God's taking too long to get back to them, so they'll make a golden idol to worship —a god more to their liking, who keeps their agenda, on their clock. It's that old problem again: Preferring the gods we make to the God Who is. Wanting a puppet godlet whose strings we can pull instead of the One who really pulls the strings.

In the next chapter, a discouraged Moses meets with God and says, *"If you are pleased with me, teach me your ways so I may know you"* (EXODUS 33:13). Then he ups the ante and says, *"Show me your glory!"* (V. 18)

Moses is asking for God's full self-disclosure. He longs for a genuine look at the core of the Creator, the depths of the Divine. Idol-free worship.

Because of what has just happened with the golden calf, I would completely expect God to answer with something like: "Moses, you have failed in your leadership miserably. You are being replaced. I am a very angry God and you humans drive me crazy. I part the Red Sea, I lead you with the fire, and this is the thanks I get?! You're gone, you're toast!"

What actually happens is this:

> *Then the* LORD *came down in the cloud and stood there with him and proclaimed his name, the* LORD. *And he passed in front of Moses, proclaiming, "The* LORD, *the* LORD, *the compassionate and gracious God, slow to anger, abounding in love and faithfulness, maintaining love to thousands, and forgiving wickedness, rebellion and sin."* EXODUS 34:5–7A

God describes Himself in the very moment of an entire nation's rebellion…

…and focuses on His *love*.

Look at each of the words God uses.

Compassionate.

The Hebrew word translated "compassionate" literally means "love rooted in a deep bond." Deep bond?! The people had basically just spit in His face! But God is talking about *His* bond of love for us. It reminds me of Jesus on the cross, loving the very people who spit at Him, insult Him, and nail Him to wood.

Gracious.

According to J. Carl Laney, the Hebrew word here means "a heartfelt response by someone who has something to give to one who has a need." It's unconditional love in action. *By it God defines Himself.*

Day 22: How God Describes Himself

Slow to anger.

Despite popular misconceptions, God does not have anger management issues. The Hebrew expression for patience used here literally means "long-nosed," referring to the tendency for your nose to get red when you're mad. God says, maybe with a trace of a smile, that it takes a long time for His face to get red! He's saying He is in no hurry to judge sinners (huge relief to me).

Abounding in love...

The specific word for "love" here means "loyal love." *I* may be disloyal. *I* may fail in my promises. *I* may prove unfaithful to my confession on any given day. Yet God is loyally loving to me through it all. In fact, the word "abounding" means He overflows with this—

and faithfulness.

Feelings of love are not much good without faithfulness. Maybe someone told you once they loved you. And they might have even meant it at the time. But they were not faithful.

I am so sorry for your pain. But I want you to know: God is not like that. He will never say, "I am just not in love with you anymore." He *abounds* in faithfulness!

And God just keeps defining Himself as One who loves:

Maintaining love to thousands and forgiving wickedness, rebellion and sin.

I love that word *maintaining*. God's love is not just a noun; it's a verb. He actively keeps a steady supply of love going to the wicked, rebellious, and sinful.

He doesn't just *feel* love; He *does* love.

One scholar says the word "thousands" means "thousands of *generations*" so this means He is the source of love to all people in history.

Of course God also explains later in these verses that there will be consequences to sin. Listen well, because these are words of warning from One who loves you: Those consequences will be felt not only by you, but may ripple out to your family, perhaps even for generations.

Because you love, you warn your children.

Because God loves, God warns His children.

But again, what is the *big picture?* In word after word, in His great self-revelation to Moses, God focuses on His infinite, loyal, faithful, love in action!

This, He says, is His glory.

What's your response to all that?

When Moses hears this, the Bible says he *"bowed to the ground at once and worshiped."* (EXODUS 34:8)

God reveals the most important thing to know about Himself: He loves us. And Moses loves Him back.

The most important thing you can know is that God loves you.

And the most important thing you can do is love Him back.

What other response is appropriate when I hear the God of the Universe emphasizing, not His power, or even merely his objective presence, but His *love*? To *me*?

To *me*, the one who has fashioned idols when I thought God was taking too long to get back to me.

To me, the one who with that crowd at the base of the mountain has at times worshipped the stupid golden calf of pleasure or prestige or possessions or (most insidiously) pride of religious performance.

To me, to you, God suddenly appears in His glory and unexpectedly announces... His powerful love.

Wow. As you study the love of God this week, may you too be moved as Moses was—to bow and worship!

God is... love.

QUESTIONS FOR REFLECTION:

What intrigues, impresses, or surprises you about God's self-description in Exodus 34:1–10?

What difference does it make for you to believe these things are true of God?

HE CAME TO MY RESCUE

READ YOUR BIBLE: *John 1:1–18*

SPOTLIGHT VERSE: *So the Word became human and lived here on earth among us. He was full of unfailing love and faithfulness. And we have seen his glory, the glory of the only Son of the Father.* JOHN 1:14

I WAS READING ABOUT the famous philosopher Friedrich Nietzsche and found a twist to his tale that surprised me. [42]

As a kid he was very involved in church. Then at 18 he rejected the faith of his deeply religious family, especially his mother.

He despised Christianity as "the religion of the weak," and promoted instead the "will to power." He wrote the book *Man and Superman.* Nietzsche insisted he and his followers were the new supermen, beyond mere notions of good and evil. They were—he said—the new gods.

Day 23: He Came To My Rescue

In fact, Nietzsche predicted that in the future, history would no longer be divided into *before Christ* and *after Christ*, but *before Nietzsche* and *after Nietzsche*.

Didn't quite work out that way.

His mind began to break down. His health too. He began to go blind. Then his friends put him in an insane asylum.

And it was at that dark hour his Christian mother re-entered his life. She'd heard about what happened and came to claim him and take him home.

Her boy had rejected her — and everything she loved. But she took him into her arms and devoted the rest of her life to his care. And people who visited would sometimes see her rocking to sleep the broken body of this man who had claimed to be a superman.

Who was *he*, that *she* should be mindful of him?

He didn't do anything to make himself lovable. In fact, he was incapable of it as his mental health deteriorated. What logical reason was there for her to love him?

This kind of love cannot be explained by logic. He was her *child*. She loved him with unwavering, unconditional love.

Like Nietzsche's mother, God comes looking for us.

He knows we are incapable of seeking Him in any way that leads to freedom. He weeps that we are locked in a prison of our own making.

So He uses all the power at His command, the same amazing power that made the Universe, to come near, to be born into our mess, to enter the asylum that is our world. And He embraces us. And takes us home.

If God's greatest self-description was to Moses, then His ultimate self-revelation was when He went beyond the middlemen, past the prophets, and came *Himself.*

The Apostle Paul puts it this way:

> *Christ is the visible image of the invisible God. He existed before everything else began, and he holds all creation together... and by him God reconciled everything to himself...* COLOSSIANS 1:15, 17

The One who created became a part of the creation. Jesus Christ is God in the flesh, which is what the word "incarnate" literally means.

The indescribable, infinite, invisible One came to earth in a form that was describable, finite, observable. To rescue you.

> *The Son reflects God's glory, and everything about him represents God exactly.* HEBREWS 1:1–3

Jesus shows you what God is like!

> When Jesus walked around on earth and patted the heads of babies, forgave harlots, and blessed mankind, He was simply God acting like God in a given situation. — A.W. Tozer [43]

God acting like God.

Want to know what God is like?

Day 23: He Came To My Rescue

You can see His power in His creation. But look what Jesus shows you. There's God...

> Hanging out with the prostitutes and lepers,
> reprimanding the priests and religious teachers,
> passionately outspoken about His love for the lost,
> very angry over religious legalism,
> delighted with children,
> healing the sick,
> giving rest to the weary.

THE ATTRIBUTES OF GOD EXPRESSED IN THE INCARNATION

Think of the God you've come to know in this study. Absolutely powerful. Perfectly present. And infinitely loving.

To me, if these are all true, then the incarnation follows. God had the means and the motive.

If God is unlimited in power, all about closeness, and perfect in love, He would be *able* to come near—and He would *want* to come near. Not only to *show* us the way, but to *be* the way.

In fact, it is precisely in the life, death, and resurrection of Jesus that I see God's power and presence and love most clearly.

I think any search-and-rescue story, like the one about Nietzsche's mom, touches me because it reflects this even greater cosmic rescue mission: God powerfully and lovingly comes to rescue you and me, at His expense, when our attempts at being god fail.

He calls your name.
He longs to hold you again.

Day 23: He Came To My Rescue

Not because you have impressed Him.
Not because you have met His expectations.
Not because you are a Super-Man or Super-Woman.
But because *He is love.*

God is… my Rescuer.

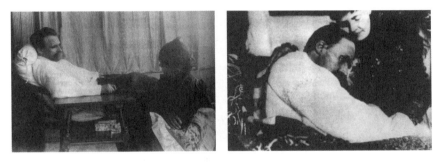

Friedrich Nietzsche and his mother

QUESTIONS FOR REFLECTION:

How does it impact you to think that the all-powerful God is also all-loving?

What does it show us about God's character that He came into the world the way He did, and then behaved the way He did, as Jesus Christ?

Each day for the rest of this week, ask yourself these two questions: Have I thanked God for His love to me today? Have I shown love to someone today?

FOR GOD SO LOVED

READ YOUR BIBLE: *John 3:1–17*

SPOTLIGHT VERSE: *For God loved the world so much that he gave his one and only Son, so that everyone who believes in him will not perish but have eternal life.*
JOHN 3:16 (NLT)

SEVERAL YEARS AGO LAURIE and I were returning from a long vacation. We were expecting our first child and after we landed in the U.S. for a customs check Laurie just really wanted to get on the next plane to go home.

But when we got to the customs line the wait was unusually long and it looked like we were going to miss our connection home.

I told her, "Hey, cheer up—maybe the airline will give us a free night in a hotel if we miss our connection! We can have a romantic night in the city!" She was tired and sick and looked at me like, "If you continue being happy about that possibility I may be forced to kill you."

Day 24: For God So Loved

So I scurried to the customs official and dared to say, "Look, I know this is out of the ordinary but my wife is pregnant—and between us, she is possibly homicidal right now—and we need to make our flight, so can you bump us to the front of the line so we can make the connection?"

He responded, "Hmmm." And I don't know why he asks me this next, but he says, "What's your job?"

I said, "Well, I'm a pastor."

And he said, "Riiiight. You have no idea how often people try to use that line." And then he challenged me: "If you're really a pastor, recite John 3:16." Like it was his fail-safe! As if no one but a pastor could possibly know this!

He folded his arms and looked at me. I glanced back. My wife was looking at me. And I thought, "I'm gonna choke! I'll end up spitting out the Gettysburg Address or something!" So I took a deep breath... and recited...

> *"For God so loved the world that he gave his one and only Son, that whoever believes in him shall not perish but have eternal life."*

And he said, "Wow, you *must* be a pastor! Move to the front of the line, Reverend!"

We got home on time. But it was no prodigious feat of memory. Of course I knew John 3:16—as a church kid, I learned it before Kindergarten. It must be the very first verse that anyone growing up in Sunday School is taught. And it's a good one.

Only problem: It suffers from what I call the "Pledge of Allegiance factor."

Ever really listen to kids saying the Pledge? Usually it's just a string of sounds that you suspect make no sense to the kids at all, something like:

> I pledge all agents to the flag of the United States of a miracle, and total reap puppets four witch it's sands, won Asian, under guard, with libber tea and just its fur all.

The same might be said of the truths in John 3:16. We know each syllable, the very cadence, so well, the words can lose their meaning.

So check this out: This may seem obvious, but John 3:16 is set up by the verses that come right before it, John 3:14–15:

> *"Just as Moses lifted up the snake in the desert, so the Son of Man must be lifted up, that everyone who believes in Him may have eternal life."*

Uh... Moses lifting up a snake? That's referring to a strange story in Numbers 21. In that passage the Israelites are in the desert, dying from poisonous snakebites. There is no antidote.

So God tells Moses He's going to do a miracle.

He instructs Moses to make a brass symbol of a snake, put it on a pole and lift it high, and anyone who merely looks on it in faith will be healed by God's grace.

Notice the artistic way our creative God heals: He turns the very symbol of death, the poisonous snake, into a symbol of hope and healing.

That healing symbol, by the way, is where we get the caduceus, the symbol for physicians in our society today.

See the parallels to you and me?

The Bible says we're dying of a poison in our soul. So Jesus is sacrificed on a cross, lifted up for all humans to see. If we look on that act in faith, we are healed. It's a beautiful, artistic, creative, loving act of grace from God. The cross, the very icon of death, becomes a symbol of hope and healing.

Now that you know the background, look again at the well-known words:

For God. The same omnipotent and majestic and holy God you've been studying.

So loved. He didn't just look on in amusement or anger or apathy. He deeply, passionately, wildly, expensively *loved*.

The world. Every child. Every man and woman. Every law-giver and law-enforcer. Every criminal and con-man. Every terrorist and every missionary. Me. You.

He gave. Not He demanded. Not He received. Not He expected. He *gave*. It's always all about what God gives, not what I do. That's grace. When you think about it, there really could be no other way *but* grace: What could I possibly do to merit anything from an infinite God?

His Son. He didn't just give a set of principles. The Father gave His one and only Son.

That whoever believes does not perish from the poison. Not whoever works real hard. Not whoever proves himself. Not whoever prays the most. Whoever *believes*.

It's that simple.

Really? Yes, really. The Israelites didn't have to know how exactly the poison's effect was counteracted when they looked up. It just was.

You don't have to know exactly how it works either.

To paraphrase A.W. Tozer, we're saved by His death, but how are we saved by His death? We're alive by His resurrection, but how are we alive by His resurrection? At some point it's just a miracle. Unfathomable. And we simply stand and gaze at the cross and whisper, "Thank you."

The Apostle Paul seems to be paraphrasing John 3:16 when he says,

> *But God showed his great love for us by sending Christ to die for us while we were still sinners.*
> ROMANS 5:8

This is the invasion God had been planning for millennia, the incident all history had been building to. God chose a moment in time to enter our world physically.

Not merely to teach or punish or model. But to save.

And God did it all because He *"loved the world so much…"*

God is… the One who loves the world.

QUESTIONS FOR REFLECTION:

How does this chapter expand your understanding of John 3:16?

I presume there were people back in Numbers 21 who refused to look at the bronze snake to be healed, because the Bible talks about those who died. In their pride they refused the grace that could have been theirs. Why would people do that? Do you ever see that tendency in yourself?

I encourage you to look to Jesus Christ as your Savior. Thank Him for His love. If you have already received this gift, pray that others may receive Christ through this study of God's attributes.

WHAT GOD FEELS FOR ME

READ YOUR BIBLE: *1 John 4:7–19*

SPOTLIGHT VERSE: *For the Lord your God has arrived to live among you. He is a mighty Savior. He will rejoice over you with great gladness. With his love, he will calm all your fears. He will exult over you by singing a happy song.* ZEPHANIAH 3:17

We forget so quickly that we are God's beloved children and allow the many curses of our world to darken our hearts. Therefore we have to be reminded of our belovedness and remind others of theirs.
— Henri Nouwen

HOW DOES THE MAJESTIC, omnipotent, holy God *feel* about you?

Ever wonder about that? Do you suspect He feels disgust or regret or loathing? Look at the verbs in today's spotlight verse.

Day 25: What God Feels For Me

God *rejoices* over you. God *calms* you. God *exults* (that means He takes delight, like a proud Father) over *you*. God *sings* about you. And it's a happy song, not a dirge!

Right now, try to picture someone who makes you happy. Imagine their eyes, their touch, their laugh. Just thinking about them makes you smile. *And that is how God feels about you!*

CAUGHT UP IN THE RAPTURES OF LOVE

Paddy Chayefsky wrote a play about a man named Gideon. In one scene Gideon is in the desert feeling rejected and lonely, but at night God breaks into Gideon's tent and overwhelms him with love.

And Gideon cries out in his Brooklyn accent:

"God, oh God, all night long I've thought of nuttin' but You, nuttin' but You. I'm caught up in the raptures of love, God! I wanna take you into my tent, wrap you up, and keep you... God, hey God, tell me that You love me!"

"I love you, Gideon," God answers.

"Yeah! Tell me again, God."

"I love you, Gideon."

Gideon scratches his head. "I don't understand. Why? Why do you love me?"

And God says, *"I hardly know why myself."*

That line always gets a laugh from the audience watching the play. But the next line tugs the heart. God says, *"But then passion is an unreasonable thing."* [44]

Day 25: What God Feels For Me

God's passion for you and for me really is *unreasonable* in the sense that cannot be explained by *reason*. It is rooted not in *reason* but in the truth that *God is love.* (1 JOHN 4:8)

And that includes the joy, the songs, the compassion, the hard choices and sacrifices of real love. *We love because He first loved us.* Amazingly, when I'm enraptured by God's love I am only mirroring what He feels for me!

WHAT GOD CALLS ME

Another place God's feelings about you are revealed: His terms of endearment for you. Did you know that God calls you His "Beloved"?

The Bible says you are:

> *...the elect of God, holy and beloved...* COLOSSIANS 3:12 (KJV)
>
> *...**beloved** of the Lord.* 2 THESSALONIANS 2:13 (KJV)

"Beloved." It's a word used most frequently in the old King James Version. And to my mind it's a better word than the more modern yet curiously formal-sounding "well loved" or "dear friends" in newer translations.

What's more, Jesus tells the church in Revelation that, in the new heaven and new earth, we'll get a name change!

When I was a kid hearing schoolyard taunts about my name, "René Schlaepfer," this was one of the aspects of heaven I looked forward to the most! I can't tell you how many times I heard, "René? That's a girl's name!" or "Shlepping around again, eh, Schlaepfer?" or "Hey, Shleprock!" *A new name? Yes!*

Maybe you were called something on the playground, or at home, that was a put-down, too. And it stung: "Loser."

Day 25: What God Feels For Me

"Disappointment." "Stoner." "Rebel." Maybe that even became a secret, internal name that, in your mind, partly defines you, even as an adult.

Now look how God changes your name in this heavenly scene:

> *I will write on them the name of my God and the name of the city of my God, the new Jerusalem...* REVELATION 3:12

So—I get the name of a *city?* Wow. "Glad to meet you, I'm Jerusalem Schlaepfer." Not much of an improvement. But wait. What is the name of the city of God?

God reveals it to Isaiah:

> *Never again will you be called "The Forsaken City" or "The Desolate Land." Your **new name** will be "The City of God's Delight" and "The Bride of God," for the LORD delights in you and will claim you as his bride.* ISAIAH 62:4 (NLT)

Do you ever feel as if you could be nicknamed, "Forsaken..."; "Desolate..."?

Well, there's a name change in store. And one of your new forever names as part of God's people will be *"God's Delight."* Sounds like a pet name someone gives their closest loved one.

And that's exactly what it is.

The God of all power cherishes you, treasures you. *Delights in you.* Don't try to say it doesn't make sense. *Passion is unreasonable.*

Day 25: *What God Feels For Me*

Try this: Say *"I am God's beloved!"* out loud. Go ahead. Now try *"I am God's delight!"*

Did you say those names with a sarcastic snicker or a hesitant whisper? That's probably a sign that the concept of God's love still needs to seep down into your soul.

And letting it seep in really makes a difference:

> Let the **beloved** of the LORD **rest secure** in him, for he shields him all day long, and the one the LORD loves **rests** between his shoulders. DEUTERONOMY 33:12

> He gives His **beloved sleep.** PSALM 127:2 (KJV)

> ...**beloved** of God, called to be saints: Grace to you and **peace from God** our Father, and the Lord Jesus Christ. ROMANS 1:7 (KJV)

How does that move you?

God is... the One who calls you Beloved.

QUESTIONS FOR REFLECTION:

Is it easy or difficult for you to say "I am God's Beloved Child!" out loud? Why?

What difference do you think it would make to say or think this throughout a normal day, and really believe it?

How does it make you feel to read Zephaniah 3:17?

Are there people you know who need to know this truth? How can you help them?

Ask yourself: Have I thanked God for His love to me today?

Have I shown love to someone today?

CANDLE IN THE WIND?

READ YOUR BIBLE: *Ephesians 3:14–19*

SPOTLIGHT VERSE: *I pray that you, being rooted and established in love, may have power, together with all the Lord's holy people, to grasp how wide and long and high and deep is the love of Christ...* EPHESIANS 3:17B–18

ARTHUR MILLER, THE FAMOUS playwright, wrote about what it was like being married to Marilyn Monroe. During the filming of her last movie, *The Misfits*, he watched her sink into an abyss of depression. One night she convinced a doctor to give her yet another tranquilizer injection.

Miller stood watching his wife as she slept:

> I found myself imagining... what if she were to wake and I were able to look at her in the eyes and say, "God loves you, darling!" and what if she were able to believe it! How I wish I still had my religion and she hers. [45]

Day 26: Candle in the Wind

Paul prays something like Miller's unsaid prayer for Marilyn in today's verses:

> *I pray that you... may have power, together with all the Lord's holy people, to grasp how wide and long and high and deep is the love of Christ...*

Paul uses a great phrase to express that: The *width, length, height, and depth* of God's love! Here's one way to meditate on that:

The *width* of that love?

It takes in all your sin, all your failures, all your mistakes and regrets. All your weaknesses, all your loneliness, all your insecurities. It's wide enough to draw a circle around all of that.

The *length?*

His love lasts forever. He has loved you from before the creation of the world. And nothing you could ever do could get God to stop loving you.

Now think of the *heights* from which He came.

Our earth is just a little speck of dust in the universe: If you could travel at the speed of light, you'd shoot past the moon in a second and a half. It would take you four years to get to the nearest star. Ten thousand years to get out of our galaxy. Two million years to reach the next closest galaxy, Andromeda. And how many galaxies are there? Billions. And the Bible says our God is enthroned far above the universe.

Now think of the *depths* to which He came to show His love.

That same God came from those heights to become… a fetus. If you'd had the technology back then, you could have taken an ultra-sound of Him. And that baby became a man who absorbed the sins of the world on the cross. And He went *deeper still*. He went to the depths of hell… for you. *Because He loves you.*

He loves you.

Can I play the role for you that Arthur Miller wished he could have played for Marilyn? If you were here with me now, I would look you in the eye and tell you:

God loves you.

You are passionately loved by the powerful God!

Maybe your whole life you've felt like an outsider. You've been abandoned. You've been burned. You've wanted love. And even when you received love it wasn't satisfying.

God loves you more than you have ever loved anything or anyone. It's *His* love you've been looking for all your life.

Believe that… and it changes everything.

LOVED AND SECURE

Yesterday I visited a man from our church in the local Veteran's Administration Hospital. He fought in Viet Nam, but now he's fighting for his life. He has an aggressive cancer that has already robbed him of his ability to swallow and to speak. To communicate, he writes his thoughts down on a tablet of paper.

At the end of our visit I prayed for Him. I prayed for a cure, for a miracle—and that he would sense God's presence through this valley of the shadow of death so that he would not be afraid.

After I said, "Amen," he grabbed his pen and paper and vigorously wrote in large letters, "I AM NOT AFRAID! PERFECT LOVE CASTS OUT *ALL* FEAR!"

I looked into his eyes and saw his smile and I knew it was true.

He wrote some more: "We all have to go sometime. I am at perfect peace because I trust God implicitly."

He was rooted. He was established. In the love of God.

That man was no trembling candle in the wind. He has confidence in God, who makes him an eternal flame.

We've focused so far on the *mighty* attributes of God a lot in this study—His omnipotence, majesty, holiness... But remember, as infinitely *powerful* as God is, He is just as infinitely *loving*.

His *power* is a *loving* power. His *love* is a *powerful* love.

God is... perfect in power *and* perfect in *love!*

Day 26: *Candle in the Wind*

QUESTIONS FOR REFLECTION:

Why do you think most people struggle with really believing God loves them?

What specific difference do you think it would make if you strengthened your belief that God has steadfast, never-ending love toward you?

Ask yourself: Have I thanked God for His love to me today?

Have I shown love to someone today?

GOD WITH SKIN ON

READ YOUR BIBLE: *1 John 3:11–18*

SPOTLIGHT VERSE: *If anyone has material possessions and sees a brother or sister in need but has no pity on them, how can the love of God be in that person? Dear children, let us not love with words or speech but with actions and in truth.* 1 JOHN 3:17–18

What can the world do to a man or woman who is grounded in the love of God, who swims in the ocean of His love as a fish in the mighty sea? What can sin do? What can the world do? What can accident do?—A.W. Tozer

IN A FAMOUS ESSAY, the surgeon Richard Selzer describes a scene that he says he will never forget:

I stand by the bed where a young woman lies, her face postoperative, her mouth twisted in palsy, clownish. A tiny twig of the facial nerve, one to the muscles of her mouth, has been severed. She will be thus from now on. The surgeon had followed with religious fervor the curve of her flesh; I promise you that. Nevertheless, to remove the tumor in her cheek, I had to cut the little nerve.

Her young husband is in the room. He stands on the opposite side of the bed, and together they seem to dwell in the evening lamplight, isolated from me, private. Who are they, I ask myself, he and this wry-mouth I have made, who gaze at and touch each other so generously, so greedily? The young woman speaks.

"Will my mouth always be like this?" she asks.

"Yes," I say, "it will. It is because the nerve was cut."

She nods and is silent. But the young man smiles.

"I like it," he says. "It is kind of cute."

All at once I *know* who he is. I understand, and I lower my gaze. One is not bold in an encounter with a god. Unmindful, he bends to kiss her crooked mouth, and I am so close I can see how he twists his own lips to accommodate to hers, to show her that their kiss still works. [46]

When he calls the man a god, he means he is acting God-like. In the incarnation, God became like us—twisting His own lips—to show His love. His love did not remain merely an *emotion*; it was put *into motion*.

One night a young mother was comforting her preschool aged daughter during a thunderstorm. "Go back to bed,

143

sweetheart," she said. And she heard the response every parent has heard from a frightened child: "I want you to be with me."

"Go to bed," said the mother, "God is with you."

"I know He is," replied the little girl, "But I want someone with skin on."

In Jesus, God put skin on. He adjusts his kiss to love the human race.

LOVING AS GOD LOVES

And now God asks you and me to love others as He loves us. To go the distance to those in need and *show* love, not merely *feel* love. To *express* God's love, not just *experience* God's love.

> *No one has ever seen God. But if we love each other, God lives in us, and his love has been brought to full expression through us.* 1 JOHN 4:12

How do you do that? I think of people in the church I serve. Their examples could fill another book.

I think of Mary, who despite her own health struggles coordinates a team of volunteers to visit men and women in nursing homes, hold weekly worship services, throw parties, and simply love them.

I think of Jack, who in his retirement has plunged into our food pantry ministry, each week leading a team that gives out bags of groceries for free to whoever's hungry.

Day 27: God with Skin On

I could tell you about divorce recovery workshops, medical and dental teams that journey to villages in India and Africa, volunteers washing the feet of the homeless, an entire team that cooks food for shut-ins, grief support groups, teenagers who help at the Rescue Mission downtown, pregnancy resource centers for frightened and often unemployed women, guys who give up two weekends every month to be dads to kids without dads, mechanics who give up their Saturdays to do free car repair for widows and the elderly, and much, much more... all just in our church.

And the scene at our church is repeated across our county and state and nation and world.

I know, the problems seem so big. But remember: there's a whole Body out there. You are one part. What is God calling *you* to do?

MY PASSION

My own heart has been captured by feeding the hungry.

Why? For one thing, it's specifically mentioned hundreds of times in the Bible as a concern of God.

Like in Isaiah 58, where God criticizes the people for having nice religious services but no real ministry. One example He specifically gives: *"I want you to share your food with the hungry..."* (ISAIAH 58:7A)

Or in the parable of the sheep and goats, where Jesus tells the sheep that they fed Him when He was hungry. They're confused. When did they ever feed Jesus? He answers that it was when they fed *"the least of these."*

Why would God place such an emphasis on feeding the hungry?

Because hunger is tied into almost every single scourge of society.

Check out these facts:

- Even mild under-nutrition can lead to reduced body and brain development.

- Kids without adequate food are more likely to get sick. And have a much higher risk of later developing diabetes, high blood pressure, cardiovascular disease, and many other illnesses.

- Kids without enough food are more likely to repeat a grade.

- Hunger in childhood is the most consistent predictor of learning problems and criminal behavior later in life.

- Hunger in childhood is also the most consistent predictor of job problems and income insecurity later in life. [47]

So: Crime, learning problems, job problems, bad health, are all tied into hunger in childhood. This is all from recent research, but of course God already knew this!

By one count, over 200 times in the Bible He says, *"Feed the hungry!"*

I don't know about you, but if God says to do something 200 times, I'm doing it.

And it costs so little. I encourage you to get involved with your church food pantry ministry, or with a local food bank.

WHEN YOU CARE YOU GET TO SHARE

One beneficial side effect of loving in incarnational ways:

When people see Christ-followers loving others, they are interested in what we have to say. As our church has raised its profile through food ministry and other community outreaches, I have had amazing chances to share God's love with people ranging from homeless men to mayors of cities and CEOs. When you care, you get chances to share.

God is… calling you to love like He loves!

QUESTIONS FOR REFLECTION:

In 1 John 3:11–18, what does the Bible say about those who claim to love God?

What are some practical ways you can love with actions and truth, and not just words, this week?

Ask yourself the following questions:
Have I thanked God for His love for me today?

Have I shown love to someone today?

DISTRACTED FROM HIM BY IT

READ YOUR BIBLE: *Mark 7:1–7*

SPOTLIGHT VERSE: *These people honor me with their lips, but their hearts are far from me.* MARK 7:7A

"I TRIED CHRISTIANITY AND it doesn't work."

"I don't know how to do it."

"It's too hard."

I listened as the man unloaded his frustrations in my office. Then I wrote down those phrases on a piece of paper as he watched.

"Look at the sentences you've been repeating," I told him. "What's the most common word here?"

He looked at the paper and answered: *"It."*

"There's your trouble," I said, paraphrasing David Seamands, one of my favorite Bible teachers and a man who'd helped me through my own struggles with legalism. "The Christian life is not an *'it.'* The Christian life is Christ: A real relationship with God!"

In today's passage Mark describes how meticulously the religious leaders of his day observed their traditions. They were very religious. But Jesus quotes Isaiah and says,

> *Their hearts are far from me. They worship me in vain; their teachings are merely human rules.*
> MATTHEW 15:8B, 9

They were distracted from Him by It. Focused on the religion, not the relationship.

It's the same criticism Christ makes later of the Ephesian Christians. He tells them He has seen their good deeds, their hard work, their high standards, how they cannot even tolerate any wicked people...

> *Yet I hold this against you: You have forsaken your first love.* REVELATION 2:4.

Very religious. No relationship.

That's why, when asked by religious leaders to name the greatest commandment, Jesus answers:

> *"Love the Lord your God with all your heart and with all your soul and with all your mind." This is the first and greatest commandment. And the second is like it: "Love your neighbor as yourself." All the Law and the Prophets hang on these two commandments.* MATTHEW 22:37–40

For God it's all about love.

"Love the Lord your God with all your heart and with all your soul and with all your mind." Please don't let this study turn into an autopsy of God, a lifeless examination of words about Him. Love Him with your mind... *and* your heart and soul. Let revelation reignite that first love for God. As you learn more of what the Bible says, let it *add* to the mystery and the awe-inspired love, instead of subtract.

"This is the first and greatest commandment." Jesus says all the other commands *follow it*. That's because the only effective way for people to change their behavior is not for them to try hard to change their behavior. People change when they fall in love.

"Love your neighbor as yourself." When I love God because I see that He loves me first, I want to love others in practical, life-changing ways, precisely the way God loves me.

At our church a woman named Lisa makes gift baskets for disabled veterans. One Valentine's Day she put together packages full of donated gifts for female vets recovering from horrible trauma—and tucked this letter inside each one:

> Hi, my name is Lisa. I haven't served our country (I cannot thank you enough for that) but I have had more than my share of unenviable experiences. I grew up in chaos and then found the same in my adult life. I have countless exterior scars and far deeper ones on my soul... But I have found healing and wholeness from God himself!

These baskets have a ton of love in them; your cards were made by the children—and signed by the members of Twin Lakes.

You have to know how much you're loved —and especially how special and precious you are to God... I really do hope you enjoy them and the dinner; *you are beautiful and cherished!*

When you know how beautiful and cherished and precious and special and loved you are to God, your heart overflows with love for Him and for others!

God is... not an It.

QUESTIONS FOR REFLECTION:

Do you ever get distracted from Him by "It"? How?

Ask yourself: Have I thanked God for His love to me today?

Have I shown love to someone today?

Be ready to share with others how God's love has overflowed in your life this week—perhaps in moments of pure worship or insight, or in opportunities to show practical acts of love to others!

GOD IS

Omniscient

It is a great consolation to me that God knows instantly, effortlessly, and perfectly all matter and all matters, all causes and all relations, all effects and all desires, all mysteries and all enigmas, all things unknown and hidden. There are no mysteries to God.

A. W. TOZER

GOD ONLY KNOWS

READ YOUR BIBLE: *Hebrews 4:12–16*

SPOTLIGHT VERSE: *Nothing in all creation is hidden from God's sight. Everything is uncovered and laid bare before the eyes of Him to whom we must give account.* HEBREWS 4:13

HAVE YOU SEEN THE Far Side comic captioned "God on Jeopardy"? A bearded man in a white robe has 85 million points, and the other two contestants are looking very peeved as Alex Trebek announces, *"And God wins again!"*

The attribute of God I want to focus on now: God is *omniscient.*

That word is a combination of *omni* which means *everything*, and *scient*, from the same root as our word *science*. God knows *everything*.

When I try to imagine the omniscience of God, I tend to think something like the image in that comic: "God has the biggest brain in the universe." He knows all the trivia about

154

the galaxies: The circumference of the sun. The speed of each comet. The light years from earth to each star system. He knows it all!

Is that all God's omniscience amounts to?

In the classic 17th-century work *The Existence and Attributes of God*, Stephen Charnock has a great meditation called, *"What Does God Know?"* His first point is the one that really blows my mind. He says the most overlooked implication of God's omniscience is this:

GOD KNOWS ALL ABOUT *HIMSELF*

Complete self-knowledge is only true of God! As H.G. Wells' angel rightly said, my little box of brains cannot hold the truth about God; it can't even hold the truth about *myself!* That's one reason I have so many problems! Someone said, "I am constantly surprising myself by doing things I thought I'd never do!" Yet God knows *Himself* fully, the only being with perfect self-knowledge.

GOD KNOWS ALL ABOUT *NATURE*

Genesis 1:21 says that after creation, *"God saw everything He had made and said, 'It is good.'"* That's an amazing statement—God saw *everything*.

Let your imagination zoom out from smallest to largest: Every atom, every molecule, every pebble, every rock, every tree, every forest, every mountain range, every planet, every star, every galaxy, every universe. He saw *everything*.

Now zoom in again.

Jesus said every time a sparrow falls to the ground, God notices.

Zoom in closer.

Jesus said God knows the exact number of hairs on your head. (For some of you guys, that's not hard, because the number is about... five. But for many people, that's amazing!)

Zoom in even more.

Jesus said God knows the number of *every grain of sand*.

Do you see a similarity with every illustration Jesus uses? All those things change, all the time. The point: God knows about everything that exists, *even as those things are constantly changing.*

GOD KNOWS ALL ABOUT *THE PAST, PRESENT, AND FUTURE*

Nothing is news to God. He knows every action and every thought that will lead to every action.

All this is stunning. But as you'll see this week, what amazes David most in Psalm 139 is that God knows all about *you*.

GOD KNOWS ALL ABOUT YOU

The idea of God seeing and knowing everything about you may not be entirely comfortable for you! So for the next few days let's explore how God's omniscience means *good* things!

Day 29: God Only Knows

To get you started, look at today's passage from Hebrews. It starts with a head-spinning description of God's omniscience:

> *Nothing in all creation is hidden from God's sight. Everything is uncovered and laid bare before the eyes of him to whom we must give account.* HEBREWS 4:13

And then look at the very practical, beautiful application! Because God knows everything, what does that mean about my relationship to Jesus?

> *...we do not have a high priest who is unable to sympathize with our weaknesses... Let us then approach the throne of grace with confidence, so that we may receive mercy and find grace to help us in our time of need.* HEBREWS 4:15A,16

You might think that because God knows everything—your temptations, your weaknesses, your motives, your thoughts—it makes Him more scary. But the Bible says this means He *sympathizes*.

You can approach God with *confidence!* Why?

God is... the One who knows!

QUESTIONS FOR REFLECTION:

Summarize in a short sentence the meaning of the omniscience of God:

If people do not really focus on the fact that God is omniscient, what false ideas or negative emotions could they potentially have?

REMEMBER THE DUCK

READ YOUR BIBLE: *Psalm 139:1–3*

SPOTLIGHT VERSE: *For a man's ways are in full view of the Lord, and He examines all his paths.* PROVERBS 5:21

IMAGINE IF EVERY SINGLE thought you had hovered above your head like the text balloons in comic strips. Would you have a single friend left by the end of one day?!

Yet David says in Psalm 139 that God knows every one of those thoughts. I don't know about you, but at first this makes me not worshipful but... uncomfortable... awkward... queasy. God knows the ugliness in my heart?

How is it *good* news to me that God knows *everything?*

I love the story of the boy and girl visiting their grandparents on their farm. On the first day there, the little boy, Johnny, gets a slingshot to play with, but he's never able to hit anything he aims at. Getting a little discouraged, he heads back to the house for lunch.

Day 30: Remember the Duck

It's then that he sees his grandma's pet duck. On an impulse, Johnny lets a pebble fly, and hits the duck—and kills it instantly. He's shocked. In a panic, he hides the dead duck in a woodpile, thinking no one will ever know! But then he looks up to see his big sister watching. Lisa had seen it all. But she says nothing. She just nods and quietly goes into the house for dinner.

After dinner Grandma says, "Kids, let's wash the dishes." But Lisa replies, "Grandma, Johnny told me he wants to help in the kitchen today alone, didn't you Johnny?" And then she whispers to him, *"Remember the duck."* So Johnny does the dishes.

Later, Grandpa asks if the kids want to go to the park, and Grandma said, "I'm sorry, but I need Lisa to help with dinner since Johnny did the lunch clean-up." But Lisa smiles and said, "Well, that's all right because Johnny told me he wanted to help you again." And she leans over and whispers to him, *"Remember the duck."* So Lisa goes outside to play and Johnny stays home.

After a full day of Johnny doing both his chores and Lisa's, he finally can't stand it any more. He confesses through tears to Grandma that he killed her duck.

She kneels down, gives him a big hug, and says, "Sweetheart, I know that. I saw you from the kitchen window. Because I love you, I already forgave you. I wondered just how long you'd let Lisa make a slave of you."

NO NEED TO HIDE

Okay, that story creeps me out a little about Lisa. But it also reminds me of my own life!

Sometimes I think I have to hide my sin, or even my sinful longings, from God. The truth is, I am encouraged to do so by an evil spiritual force. The Bible has an interesting name for the devil: The Accuser. That's the condemning voice that whispers, "Why do you think you could ever hope to get close to God? He can't stand you. Look at you. Think of all you've done. *Remember the duck!*"

Yet there is no need to let the Accuser frighten you away from a full confession to God. He's just trying to make a slave of you.

God's omniscience means that when I fall, I can avoid the common trap of denial and hiding, since nothing is hidden from God anyway. I can go skip those steps and go straight to admitting my sin before Him.

God's omniscience means my confession doesn't surprise Him. He never says, "You did WHAT?!" God is not shocked by my sin. He saw it coming. You don't confess to inform God, but to return to the One who loves you.

In fact, God's omniscience means God not only knows *what* happened; God knows *why* it happened. God is the most genuinely sympathetic listener you'll ever have, and He is the most amazingly effective counselor you'll ever have too.

> *If our hearts condemn us, we know that God is greater than our hearts, and he knows everything.*
> 1 JOHN 3:20 (NLT)

GOD UNDERSTANDS YOU

Maybe you've been saying "No one understands me" for so long that you believe it. But to say God is omniscient means not only that God *knows* you completely. It means God *understands* you completely. And God can heal you. Completely.

Have you ever played hide and seek with really little kids? They stash themselves behind a bed or in a closet, and the whole time they're hiding, you know very well where they are.

Once I played hide and seek with my daughter Elisabeth when she was very young, and I searched for so long that she began to cry. She thought I would never find her, and she'd have to stay hidden forever! When I heard her whimpering I said, "Elisabeth, come out, come out, wherever you are!" And when she emerged she found me steps away, on my knees with my arms open, ready to embrace her.

God's omniscience means you can stop hiding.

God knows right where you are. And God waits to welcome you with open arms.

God is... the One who understands me.

QUESTIONS FOR REFLECTION:

How does an awareness of God's omniscience help me get on the path of recovery more quickly following a fall?

Do you ever try to "hide" from God, or least try to avoid Him? Why?

What difference does it make for you to really believe that God *understands* you?

DAY 31
SOMEONE KNOWS AND SOMEONE CARES

READ YOUR BIBLE: *Psalm 139:4–6, 17–18*

SPOTLIGHT VERSE: *Before a word is on my tongue, you, Lord, know it completely.* PSALM 139:4

THERE WAS A POPULAR commercial a while back that showed a middle-aged receptionist punching a switchboard in a white room:

"Hello, this is heaven."

"Shark!!"

"I'll put you right through! Hello, this is Heaven..."

"Yeah, I'm being investigated for tax fraud..."

"Please hold, Senator... Heaven..."

"Yeah, my daughter's marrying a rock musician."

"Oh, I'll connect you right away!"

When I pray I can find myself acting a little like that: It's all about informing God. *"Lord, here's the René report..."*

Earlier I quoted from a book called *Children's Letters to God*. In another of these actual letters from children, a little boy fills God in on his life:

> Dear God: My name's Simon. That's from the Bible. I am eight and a half. We live across the street from the park. I have a dog named Buster. I used to have a hamster but he got out and ran away. I am small for my age. My hobbies are swimming, bowling, my chemistry set, reading, coin collecting, and tropical fish. Right now I have three kinds. Well I guess I said a mouthful. Goodbye, Always a friend, Simon. [48]

I tend to pray a lot like that! I'm sure God loves every sincere word, but it's good for me to realize He doesn't need a reporter here on earth, checking in with Him.

In today's Scripture, David says that God knows all our words before they are even formed. Even half-formed prayer words like:

"I know it's wrong but I want to do it anyway."

"I feel so stupid. Why did I do that?"

"How could God love me?"

"Lord, I am so sorry."

"I am so scared."

Day 31: Someone Knows and Someone Cares

"I'm so lonely."

"I hate you."

"I love you."

"Are you real?"

He knows *every word.*

That's why Jesus said,

> *"When you pray, do not keep on babbling like pagans, for they think they will be heard because of their many words. Do not be like them, for your Father knows what you need before you ask him."*
> MATTHEW 6:7–8

Why pray, then? To reconnect with Him. To relax in Him. To release your burdens. To receive relief.

God isn't waiting for you to inform Him so He knows what's going on, or to confess to Him so He can explode at you in surprised rage, because, remember, nothing surprises Him. He's waiting for you to come to Him so that He can restore the vitality of your relationship.

During those times when you think, "Nobody knows and nobody cares," you can rest assured—*Someone* knows. And that Someone cares.

QUESTIONS FOR REFLECTION:

This week, repeat this phrase to yourself often: *"Someone knows and Someone cares."* How does it positively impact you to remind yourself of this truth?

Although you may believe in God's omniscience intellectually, does your behavior demonstrate your trust in that truth?

HE NEVER MISSES A HIGHLIGHT

READ YOUR BIBLE: *Matthew 6:1–6*

SPOTLIGHT VERSE: *Then your Father, who sees what is done in secret, will reward you.* MATTHEW 6:4B

I'LL COME RIGHT OUT and say it: I'm a klutz. Sometimes I think I'm one of the most uncoordinated people on the planet. My wife, on the other hand, is extremely coordinated.

This came into play right away, on our first date. She suggested night skiing. Not just skiing. Skiing… *at night*. For me that's a recipe for disaster. I can barely walk down the *sidewalk* at night. All evening she was going off jumps, shushing down the hill, and all the while my thighs were burning as I tried to maintain the snowplow posture to the bottom of the bunny hill.

Second date, she chose… *roller skating*. She was skating backwards, doing tricks, rexing (remember that word? For the young and uninitiated, it means to dance on skates. Used

166

to be cool. Really…). Meanwhile, I was clinging to the sides of the skating rink like a frightened swimmer hanging on to the side of a pool, then flipping upside down at sudden, random intervals, my legs shooting into the air like I was Charlie Chaplin in an old movie.

The only sport I did in high school—the only sport I *could* do—was track, because it required an absolute minimum of hand-eye coordination. The coach would say: "René, listen carefully. When the man in the hat fires the gun, run! Run like the wind!" *"Okay, coach!"*

One day our mile relay group needed a runner for one of the four legs of their race because flu had hit the team, and I was the only one available, much to the coach's chagrin. Looking back, I realize a lot of people must have been sick for him to trust me with this! He wisely spent quite a long time telling me how to hold the baton, which had to be passed from one runner to the next. I have to say, that baton complicated the whole situation for me exponentially. "Run while *holding* something? Do two things at once?!" I simply couldn't multi-task! I think the coach was afraid I'd just switch my focus throughout the race: "Run. Hold. Run. Hold. Run."

Well, this acute coordination difference did not prevent me and Laurie from getting married, but for years I still tried to prove to her that I could hold my own athletically.

Early in our marriage I was a youth pastor in San Diego, and part of my job was to coach two softball teams. Me! I really had but one objective. I wanted to impress Laurie so *badly*. I wanted her to believe she had married well, that her family's athletic gene pool was not going to be watered down.

So I went to batting cages every morning. Worked on fielding each afternoon.

She came to the first game. And I immediately struck out. *In slow-pitch softball.* Which you probably couldn't do if you tried.

Next time up, I walloped one—a home run! I looked over while trotting around the bases—she was talking to some friends. She never saw it.

That became the pattern:

I'd snag a hard-hit ball (whap!), look over—she'd be at the snack bar.

I'd bobble it like a drunk juggler, drop it, look over—she'd be shaking her head, like, "Is there something wrong with you that you haven't told me about?"

After a while she just didn't come to my games anymore. It was too painful for her. But that's just when I was gettin' good!

I'd come home, "Honey, you should've seen it, I won the game! Hit a ball so far over their heads— !" She'd say, "Uh-huh." And I'm certain she was thinking, "This is so pathetic, how he's lying to me."

Obviously she somehow felt I had virtues that outweighed those faults... But have you ever been in a relationship like that with a boss or a friend or a neighbor? Every single time you do something stupid, they're right there, watching, taking notes. But do something great? They're out of town.

Sometimes I can imagine my relationship with God like that. He's omniscient. That means *He sees my every mess-up.*

But one of the things *omniscience* also means is that every time I do the *right* thing, God is watching. *He never misses a highlight.*

Think of what this means for you.

Every time you say a kind word instead of a cutting word, every time you give someone an extra moment instead of hurrying on, every time you resist a sin instead of yielding to it, every time you give someone thirsty a drink, every time you give a can of food to the church pantry, every time you visit an elderly friend in a rest home, every time you sacrifice your wants to help someone with a need, every time you smile at someone who feels awkward, every time you have a chance to be negative but stay positive—every time you help out in the smallest ways—He sees it and records it and promises to reward it.

He's never looking the other way.

Jesus said,

> *Truly I tell you, anyone who gives you a cup of water in my name because you belong to the Messiah will certainly not lose their reward.* MATTHEW 10:42

This means every good deed will be rewarded, no matter how insignificant.

Don't get me wrong: I'm not saying you need to show these things to God in order to get Him to love you. He loves you already, unconditionally. I mean to say that even when I think no one notices, He not only sees those good deeds, but He sees them as ways I am loving Him back for His love to me.

I'm saying Jesus Christ will surprise you in heaven by recounting things you did for others, things you did with mixed motives, things no one else noticed, even things that were so small you yourself forgot about them by the end of the day. But He sees. And He remembers.

GOD KNOWS

You may be a single Mom, thinking no one has any idea how hard it is to raise kids, keep up with the laundry, help with the homework, make nutritious meals, and stay spiritually focused, and sometimes you wonder: Does anyone know how hard this is? Does anyone see?

Well, God sees. And God will reward.

You might visit a loved one with Alzheimer's who doesn't even remember you were there. You get frustrated.

God sees, and He will personally thank you.

Maybe you're in a ministry with very little appreciation-level. Thank-you cards are rare. Personal sacrifices are many. Resentment sometimes builds up.

But God knows what you're doing. He sees every long night and every personal sacrifice, and your reward in heaven will far surpass any earthly toys you're giving up here.

In fact, Jesus says in Matthew 6 that this means you don't have to worry at all about impressing anyone... ever! What freedom!

I love the saying "live for an audience of one" because it takes away so much pressure. Who cares what others think? God is cheering me on.

God is... the One who never misses a highlight.

QUESTIONS FOR REFLECTION:

When do you struggle with feeling unappreciated?

How does it help you to know that God's omniscience means not just that He sees you when you fall, but that He sees all the highlights too, and promises to reward them all—even the little things that you will likely forget?

THE ONE WHO SEES

READ YOUR BIBLE: *Psalm 33:13–22*

SPOTLIGHT VERSE: *From His throne He observes all who live on the earth. He made their hearts, so He understands everything they do.* PSALM 33:14–15 (NLT)

TAKE A GOOD LOOK at the Scripture reading for today and notice all the ways the Psalmist describes God's omniscience:

The Lord *looks... sees... observes... understands... watches...*

But... why?

When I was a kid devouring every comic book I could get my hands on, there was a character in the *Fantastic Four* series called The Watcher. He was an omniscient being who lived on the moon, and could see everything humans did. He knew it all. But he was allowed to do *nothing* about it. He merely watched... observed... knew...

That's the picture of God a lot of people have. Like Bette Midler sang: "God is watching us. From a distance."

But God's omniscience is not like that. He sees... and He helps.

THE LIVING ONE WHO SEES

A single mother many ages ago experienced this: Hagar, in the Bible.

In fact, this handmaid of Sarah had her own intriguing, personal name for God.

The Bible says,

> *She gave this name to the* LORD *who spoke to her:* "*You are* **the God who sees me,**" *for she said,* "*I have now seen* **the One who sees me.**" GENESIS 16:13

I have to wonder why this name for God meant so much to Hagar.

Maybe she was used to being invisible.

Perhaps because she was the handmaid, the servant, the help, people just sort of looked right through her. She was not *seen* as much as *used*. Even Abraham essentially used her to bear a son.

But somewhere she learned about God. And of all the attributes of God that might have impressed Hagar, she is moved most by the mere fact that God, the ruler of all, *sees her*.

He sees her! He notices her need, validates her existence, acknowledges her dignity and worth.

She even names a well in the desert after God; she calls it *"The well of* **the Living One who sees me.***"*

Then later, in beautiful wordplay, when Hagar and her son are about to starve in the desert, alone, the Bible says God "opened her eyes" and *she* sees—she sees an oasis that saves their lives.

The One who sees helped *her* see the precious oasis.

Just as the holy one makes you holy,

Just as the all-powerful one gives you power,

Just as the God of love helps you love,

so the *Living One who sees* enables *you* to see.

I have a suggestion for you: Whenever you pray today, try addressing God with Hagar's name for Him: *"You are the Living One who sees me."*

And then wait for God to open your eyes, so you see the oasis, the beauty, the rest for your soul, near you!

God is… the Living One who sees me.

QUESTIONS FOR REFLECTION:

When have you ever felt invisible?

Try addressing God with Hagar's name for Him: "You are the Living One who sees me." What impact does this make on you?

THE POWER OF
THE HOLY SPIRIT

READ YOUR BIBLE: *John 14:16–27*

SPOTLIGHT VERSE: *And he will be called Wonderful Counselor, Mighty God, Everlasting Father, Prince of Peace.* ISAIAH 9:6B

EVERY TIME I SPEAK to an audience, I struggle with nerves. And that's kind of a drag considering that's what I do for a living. But I'll tell you a secret. I am much, much calmer than I used to be.

I was inspired by the story of Thomas Spurgeon, who followed his famous father Charles as pastor of the world's first mega-church, Metropolitan Tabernacle in London.

Charles, the dad, was a dynamo, full of charisma. He grew a church of 200 to over 8,000—and this was in the mid-1800s! He also started 17 nursing homes, 2 schools, a seminary, and an orphanage.

But when he died, his son Thomas was asked to take over. He had pastored in Australia, but was forced to retire early due to his fragile health. And now he was being asked to return to foggy London! He decided he could go in God's power, and the church prospered.

But then the fire hit.

In April 1898, the Metropolitan Tabernacle went up in flames. There were terrible casualties. Thomas was shaken to the core. Never the most self-confident man, he found himself dreading the day he would have to climb the stairs of the rebuilt church stage to preach for the first time. He had some sort of psychological block—real stage fright of the worst kind.

When that day came, he stood up and approached the platform. And then froze, thinking, "I cannot do this!" And he almost walked right out of the building, ready to quit.

But then he said to himself, "I can take one more step with the power of God." He prayed under his breath, "I believe in the power of the Holy Spirit." And took that one step.

Then he said it again. "I believe in the power of the Holy Spirit." And took the next step.

With each step he repeated, "I believe in the power of the Holy Spirit" until he reached the podium and preached powerfully. And he had 14 more years of wonderful ministry there.

That true story made such an impression on me that I have said that exact phrase to myself on many occasions, swallowing hard as I approach the pulpit nervously, "I believe in the power of the Holy Spirit. I believe in the power of the Holy Spirit."

In fact, it's become such an effective reminder that now my wife asks me whenever I get nervous or worried, "Do you believe in the power of the Holy Spirit?"

God is omniscient, as we've studied this week. And here is the mind-blower for today: That same omniscient God, who sees and sympathizes... is your *Mighty Counselor!*

I have found human counselors to be very helpful. But their ability to help is limited by their knowledge—their knowledge of you, and your problem. God has no such limitation. He knows you better than you know yourself! God's omniscience is not theoretical. It has very practical consequences for you.

ALWAYS BY YOUR SIDE

Jesus said,

> *"I will not leave you as orphans; I will come to you... the Counselor, the Holy Spirit, whom the Father will send in my name, will teach you all things..."*
> JOHN 14:18,26

The word translated Counselor or Advocate (depending on your Bible) is fascinating in the original Greek language. It does conjure images of someone who counsels. But it means far more than that.

The Greek word is *paraclete*. That means "one who comes alongside." It was an ancient warrior's term.

Greek soldiers went into battle in pairs, so when the enemy attacked, they could defend themselves back-to-back, covering each other's blind side. Your battle partner was your *paraclete*.

God doesn't send you out there alone. He's got your back.

And He's even closer than that: He's *within* you, empowering you to will and act according to His purpose (see Philippians 2:13).

God counsels and fights powerfully for you! You never have to worry about abandonment again.

God is... your omniscient Counselor.

QUESTIONS FOR REFLECTION:

What impact does it make on you to realize that the same God we have been studying is your *paraclete*, the One who is alongside you, guiding and guarding?

Think of the problems you are facing, the fears you have... and now repeat, "I believe in the power of the Holy Spirit." What impact does this make on you?

DAY 35

WHAT ABOUT GOD'S ANGER?

READ YOUR BIBLE: *Nehemiah 9:13–31*

SPOTLIGHT VERSE: *You are a forgiving God, gracious and compassionate, slow to anger and abounding in love.*
NEHEMIAH 9:17B

FOR MANY PEOPLE, THE omniscience of God is inevitably tied up with a fear of His judgment.

I've tried to show how, in the Bible, God's omniscience is usually related to His sympathy and mercy and reward. In fact, I've attempted to show how all of God's attributes mean good things for you. But this may seem to tiptoe around an elephant in the room: What about the passages in the Bible that talk about God's *anger?*

Whenever you do a study on the attributes of God, you run into passages about God's *wrath*. Let's face it: These verses can be very troubling—especially when His anger destroys people!

Day 35: What About God's Anger?

Linda Falter wrote a great article about this called *"A Beautiful Anger"* in *Christianity Today* magazine. As she points out, some people find the Bible passages about God's wrath to be a stumbling block to belief:

> They choose the "safer" scenario of a universe without God over one in which our lives hang on the mercy of an infinitely powerful force we can't fully understand, much less control. [49]

But is a universe without God really safer? And if there really is a God, would I understand all His motives and methods? I think not.

Regardless, it's still confusing for many. What do you do with the God of some (mostly) Old Testament passages who seems to wreak total vengeance on one group and lavish completely undeserved mercy on another?

One key is to realize that *God is always all of His attributes.* He never satisfies justice without also being holy and beautiful and loving.

The problem is, we humans usually can't imagine anger being anything but ugly.

This is another case where human words very inadequately describe God, the Wholly Other. We use words like "anger" and "wrath." But we often associate these words with *losing temper*, with going *out of control*. Because that's what *we* do.

But God's anger is not like yours or mine.

What we call "anger" in God is always infused with holy purpose. God never loses it. So even in His wrath there is compassion, love, patience.

Day 35: What About God's Anger?

Once again, the historical context is important. See the big picture:

The seemingly random acts of wrath in the Old Testament (although, if you actually chart them out, are surprisingly rare even there) are always called for, in this sense: You may be upset with God for judging those people, but first look at what those people were up to. There was vicious brutality going on that God in His justice and compassion and love was moved to stop. I have a feeling that if I were living then, I'd easily find myself on the side of people like Jonah, who wondered not why God *judges*, but why God was *waiting so long* to judge!

Plus, in the Old Testament, God's discipline is never a *surprise*. Prophets always warn the potential recipients of God's judgment.

And repentance is always a possibility. God's judgments always have a purpose: Restoration. The same hands that punish offer a pull to safety. The pronouncements of the prophets are always mixed with hope and God's desire for reconciliation.

Finally, always remember that the crucifixion reveals, to the fullest extent yet, the nature of God toward sinners. As Falter writes,

> Try to imagine it! The blameless, beloved Son of God is mocked, tortured, and murdered while his Father watches.
>
> ...Surely God would need no further justification to manifest his wrath toward evildoers. But, amazingly, this is the point at which God chooses to reveal the

strength and beauty of his holy love. The Almighty gives silent assent to the words, "Father, forgive them."

...God's silence at Jesus' suffering is the greatest of all mysteries, and sufficient to muffle all accusations of bloodthirstiness in his character. For if God is a vengeful judge, then what happened at the Cross — or rather, what did not happen — makes no sense. Surely there is no greater sin than to kill the innocent Son of God. Yet God fails to avenge him. Why? Similarly, if God's assessment of man is that we are all prisoners on death row, then why not be done with it and kill us all? [50]

It's because God is perfectly just and also infinitely merciful. It's this incomprehensibly Perfect One in whom I place my trust.

How does this tie into omniscience?

I believe God is perfectly wise and will ultimately know just how to treat us all with justice and love. God's final judgments will be unassailably perfect. Precisely because He knows all.

God is... wise and just.

QUESTIONS FOR REFLECTION:

In what ways does human anger give people a false impression of what God's anger is like?

How can God show wrath toward sin without compromising other attributes like love and grace? How was this accomplished on the cross?

WEEK 6

GOD IS

Sovereign

When you bow your head to pray, are you aware of who you're talking to? The one to whom you pray has power over the entire universe, over every single atom, and yet He is infinitely loving and He cares about you. That's who you're talking to. CHIP INGRAM

GOD IS IN CONTROL

READ YOUR BIBLE: *Romans 11:33–36*

SPOTLIGHT VERSE: *Wealth and honor come from you; you are the ruler of all things. In your hands are strength and power to exalt and give strength to all.*
1 CHRONICLES 29:12

THE LOS ANGELES TIMES recently ran this headline: "Sleeping pill use grows as economy keeps people up at night."[51] The article reports prescriptions have jumped 54% in five years. I think that's one indication anxiety is definitely on the rise.

There are others.

A dog-fancier told me the other day that poodles and Chihuahuas *used* to be the most popular dog breeds. Now? German shepherds, dobermans, and huskies!

A dentist said recently he has even observed that teeth-grinding is on the rise!

Day 36: God is in Control

Anxiety's amped up. Serenity's in short supply.

So how do you deal with those increasing worries?

Remind yourself of the truths you've been investigating so far in this study: Is anything too hard for God? No. Does God promise to be with you at all times? Yes. Does God love you infinitely? Yes. Does God know all about your troubles? Absolutely.

And here's the one that brings it home. The attribute of God you'll dig into this week. *Sovereignty*. Saying God is *sovereign* means God reigns. He's the King. God is in control.

If you're looking for a job, God is in control.

If you are waiting for a child, God is in control.

If you don't know what the doctor's test results will be, God is in control.

That means you can relax. You don't have to worry. God's in the front seat driving. He might not take you exactly where you want to go, but (after what may look like a series of detours) He'll take you to a place that's best.

That's awesome.

However. Sovereignty also makes my head hurt.

It raises obvious questions:

Does *sovereignty* mean everything that happens is in God's perfect will?

Day 36: God is in Control

It must not, or why would Jesus tell us to pray *"Your kingdom come, your will be done, on earth as it is in heaven."* (MATTHEW 6:10) If God's will is always done on earth as it is in heaven, why do I need to pray for it?

But... if His perfect will is *not* always done on earth, then does that mean He is *not* really sovereign?

Some theologians have resolved this by distinguishing between God's *permissive* will and God's *perfect* will. God permits some things that are not in his perfect design. But ultimately His perfect design will always prevail.

This may not work for you, but here's an analogy that helps me:

God is like the captain of a cruise ship.

He is piloting the vessel. He is in charge of the crew. The ship will get to wherever He wants it to go, when He wants it to get there.

We're like the passengers.

We can choose to hit or help fellow passengers, to enjoy the cruise or complain, to make a mess or keep it clean, to swim in the pool or, inexplicably, to play bingo. And the captain permits that freedom. But ultimately my choice is not going to change what the captain will do with all of us on that boat. He has our destiny in His hands.

Another metaphor: You're playing chess. With God. You are free to make all kinds of moves, to try all sorts of strategies. But since you are playing God, He will ultimately win the game.

Of course these are both imperfect analogies, but they help me work out the problem a little, and seem to match what the Bible says: The Scripture says God holds me responsible for my decisions. My choices do have consequences. Yet it says that in the end, God's purposes always prevail.

I appreciate the way John Morren puts it:

> I read the many teachings of the Bible regarding God's election, predestination, His chosen, and so on. I read also the many teachings regarding "whosoever will may come" and urging people to exercise their responsibility as human beings. These seeming contradictions cannot be reconciled by the puny human mind. With childlike faith, I cling to both ropes, fully confident that in eternity I will see that both strands of truth are, after all, of one piece. [52]

Most importantly, God apparently gives us all a choice to follow Him or not.

But why? Why should a sovereign God leave me free to choose this? Why not just make us all his puppets?

I'm not sure why, but I think it has to do with the fact that God is love, and desires a loving relationship with you and me. And it seems to me that for true love to exist, a true choice must exist. Even if those choices hurt. And they might. My choices can bring healing or they can bring suffering—not only to myself, but to others as well.

In fact, the age-old choice of humans to rebel against God so shook the foundations of God's perfect creation that it was like an atomic bomb detonation. The consequence of human rebellion against God has had an impact not only on every human's nature, but on nature itself. So now we're all living in the fallout of the sin bomb, so to speak, living with sin's consequences in a broken world.

But! Even in this world marred by sin, God's sovereign will ultimately prevails. Not only does the Bible promise that He will one day restore the earth to its perfect glory; even now God works through every tragedy to bring good. I'll have lots of examples in the devotions this week.

WONDER AND HUMILITY

I'll admit it—trying to comprehend the twin truths of human responsibility and divine sovereignty will hurt your head!

But again, if it's true, and it's about God, then that's to be expected.

That's why after three chapters of talk about God's sovereign plan in the book of Romans, Paul has to throw his hands in the air and say,

> *Oh, the depth of the riches of the wisdom and knowledge of God!*
> *How unsearchable his judgments,*
> *and his paths beyond tracing out!*
> *Who has known the mind of the Lord?*
> *Or who has been his counselor?*
> *Who has ever given to God,*
> *that God should repay them?*
> *For from him and through him and for him are all things.*
> *To him be the glory forever! Amen.* ROMANS 11:33–36

In all of my God-thoughts, I need to maintain an attitude of wonder and humility like that.

Let's talk about those implications of sovereignty this week.

God is… in control.

QUESTIONS FOR REFLECTION

What tends to make you anxious or worried? What are you anxious or worried about right now?

How does trust in God's sovereignty help overcome anxiety about these things?

GOD IS SOVEREIGN IN THE GOOD AND BAD

READ YOUR BIBLE: *Isaiah 45*

SPOTLIGHT VERSE: *I am the* LORD, *and there is no other. I form the light and create darkness, I bring prosperity and create disaster; I, the* LORD, *do all these things.*
ISAIAH 45:6B, 7

THERE'S AN OLD STORY from India about a king with an advisor who has the annoying habit of responding to any event by saying, "That's good!"

The king loses his toe in a hunting accident. The advisor says, "That's good!"

So the king fires him from his job. Keeping it consistent, the advisor says, "That's good!"

A month later the king is captured by a group of villagers who plan to use him in a sacrificial ceremony. When they find his toe is gone, they declare him unclean and let him go. Back at the palace he reinstates the advisor.

"You were right," the king says, "It was good that I lost my toe, for it saved my life today. But why did you say it was good when I fired you from your job?"

The advisor answers, "Your Highness, I cannot see the future, but I have learned to trust that some good comes from each event. Today I see what that was for me. Had you not fired me, I would have remained with you when you were captured by the tribesmen. And because I am in possession of all my fingers and toes, I would have been next in line for the sacrifice!"

SOVEREIGNTY IN THE CALAMITY

It is impossible for me, at the human level, to predict what good God can bring out of any calamity. But contained within the concept of His *sovereignty* is a promise that He will!

One weekend I left after our final church service to catch a flight to a conference. And the whole freeway to the airport was completely shut down. I had to drive surface streets. A 40-minute trip took me 2 hours. I missed the flight. Then a storm blew in, and other flights were cancelled. The only seat I could find was on another airline to another airport, from which I'd have to rent a car to drive to my destination. It was a mess, or so I thought.

I finally sat down on this late flight, and the young guy sitting next to me was from a town near our church, and we had a long conversation for the entire trip. I always wonder how people will react when I tell them I'm a pastor, but when I told him, he said, "Pastor?! I've been trying to find a pastor in town to meet with, but I didn't know anybody! Can I get your name and number so I can call you?"

And I said, "Forget it."

No, of course I didn't! I gave him my contact info. Now—do you think God worked that out? He is sovereign.

In fact, I can look back at every long-ago catastrophe in my life, including the tragic death of my father when I was just 4, and see now how God worked through those tragedies.

Can I see God's hand in every one of my more recent tough times? Not yet, but I trust that one day I will.

I don't mean to say here that God does evil things, or that evil is somehow actually good; I mean that God in His sovereignty brings really good things even out of really bad things.

HE IS THE POTTER, WE'RE THE CLAY

God can work in the weirdest ways.

That's the point, really, of today's Bible reading.

When we pick up the story, the Israelites have been captives in Babylon for decades. Then the Persians invade and conquer Babylon. Now they're still captives, only under a totally new system of government. All their old connections, their language skills, are all useless. Everything seems to be going from bad to worse.

Day 37: God is Sovereign in the Good and Bad

Then in Isaiah 45, God says He has an announcement to make: He will... judge the Persians? Set the Israelites free? No, God says He will...

...bless the new Persian ruler, King Cyrus, even though Cyrus does not even believe in God, keep the commandments, or know the Jewish law! In fact, God says Cyrus will be His "anointed," His Chosen One for that generation.

Talk about a potentially confusing message.

Anticipating complaints, God says,

> *"Does the clay dispute with the one who shapes it, saying, 'Stop, you're doing it wrong!'?"*
> ISAIAH 45:9B (NLT)

From my perch 2,600 years later, I can see how God used Cyrus in the history of Israel in some very profound ways. It was far better for them to be under Persian rule than Babylonian. In fact, Cyrus helped restore Jerusalem to its former glory.

But in the moment, the people of Israel were frustrated that God was taking the confusing step of blessing an enemy.

What tough situations do you look at in your life now—situations where you cannot imagine how anything good could ever emerge?

God essentially says, relax. In the long run this produces benefits you cannot now imagine. Just wait.

God is... working it out.

QUESTIONS FOR REFLECTION

What tough situations do you look at in your life where you cannot now imagine how anything good could ever emerge?

How have you seen God, in His sovereignty, bring good from bad situations in your past?

Write out at least two verses from Isaiah 45 that are an encouragement to you, and be ready to share them with others:

GOD IS SOVEREIGN
OVER INJUSTICE

READ YOUR BIBLE: *Psalm 75*

SPOTLIGHT VERSE: *It is God alone who judges; he decides who will rise and who will fall.* PSALM 75:7

MILLIONS WERE CAPTIVATED RECENTLY by the story of Jaycee Lee Dugard. A California girl kidnapped when she was just 11 years old, Jaycee was found alive 18 years later, living in virtual slavery in the backyard of the man who abducted her.

I knew her family.

The kidnapping happened when I was a pastor in South Lake Tahoe, and I spoke several times afterward to her stepfather and mother. People in our church helped organized meals and marches for the community group "Jaycee's Hope." A small group of us would go to coffee after letter-mailing or marching with Jaycee's mom, doing our best to encourage her and to assure her of our prayers.

One day I asked her, "How are you holding up through all of this?"

I will never forget her response. She told me, "I am clinging to the idea that ultimately God is in charge of justice here. Either He will answer our prayers and bring Jaycee back, or if that doesn't happen, He will make sure justice gets done, here or in the hereafter." She held my gaze for a moment, and then said, "I would go crazy if I did not believe that." This was many years before she was reunited with Jaycee.

The justice of God is one of the implications of his sovereignty. If I believe He rules, then I believe He will bring a fair and just resolution to all that I now see left undone. He will right every wrong, punish the evildoers, mete out retribution.

Among other things, this means I do not need to be a vigilante. He promises, *"At the time I have planned, I will bring justice against the wicked."*– PSALM 75:2

FREE FROM REVENGE

This became personal for me when I realized I still struggled with hatred against the piano teacher who molested me when I was a child. As far as I know there was never any legal action taken against him. I had long forgotten his name, but not my intense feelings of anger and fantasies of vengeance.

Finally one night, while taking the last freeway exit on the drive home, I realized I had to do something. I noticed I had a white-knuckle grip on the steering wheel and was once again imagining torturing this man in quite graphic detail.

Day 38: God is Sovereign Over Injustice

I pulled over and said, "God, You are sovereign. I don't even know this man's name anymore. I don't know how I could possibly pursue legal action against him. I have been spinning my wheels in this patch of filth for years. I hate him so much. But You are in control. You have the authority to punish, and You promise to do what is fair. I release him to You. Please let me live in hatred no longer."

Usually when I turn something I am struggling with over to God, growth is gradual and slow. But in this instance I can say that I felt an immediate relief that has endured to this day.

I'm not saying your sense of relief will be that instant. Maybe it will; maybe the struggle to forgive will take longer. You are no worse than I am if it does take longer; I was blessed in this case with what I believe to be a miracle of healing.

But if vengeance fantasies and hatred have been plaguing you, I want to encourage you to begin to give that longing for revenge to the sovereign God. At least tell Him, "I don't want to give this to You, so please help me."

Of course, if there is a way to seek legal recourse, I encourage you to do that as well—our society needs to be protected against these predators—but even then do it without hatred or vengeance.

> Do not take revenge, my dear friends, but leave room for God's wrath, for it is written: "It is mine to avenge; I will repay," says the Lord. ROMANS 12:19

God is... the ultimate Judge.

QUESTIONS FOR REFLECTION

What is the advantage to letting God avenge, in His time and in His way, rather than taking vengeance into your own hands?

Have you had any situations like René's, where you had to let go of bitterness and release the injustice to God's control? What happened? Is there a situation you're currently struggling with? How can you apply what you've learned and begin to release that situation?

GOD IS SOVEREIGN
WHEN I'M OVERWHELMED

READ YOUR BIBLE: *2 Chronicles 20:1–12*

SPOTLIGHT VERSE: *"You are ruler of all the kingdoms of the earth. You are powerful and mighty; no one can stand against you!"* 2 CHRONICLES 20:6B (NLT)

GOD IS BIGGER.

That is a sentence that is always true.

No matter what you are talking about or comparing Him to, God is bigger. God is bigger than your opponents. God is bigger than your worries. God is bigger than the problem you are facing.

But you might not always live like this is true.

Ever feel overwhelmed by problems and stresses?

Then you'll relate to the king in today's Scripture reading. It's part of a fascinating story: Three nations, enemies of

Day 39: God is Sovereign When I'm Overwhelmed

Israel, band together to bring down King Jehoshaphat. Ironically, these are the very three countries that the Israelites had been ordered by God to treat well—to never fight against. And now they're paying the Israelites back for their kindness with treachery of the worst sort.

You may relate. You may feel like problems are ganging up on you. You may be terrified, like Jehoshaphat.

What's been your strategy so far? Lying awake at night worrying? Lashing out in anger? Thinking non-stop about your problems? Trying to escape from them through amusement or substances?

How are those strategies working out for you?

Why not try Jehoshaphat's strategy?

The king of Israel is terrified, and calls a giant prayer meeting. In front of everyone, he admits his fear. And he appeals to one thing: God's sovereignty.

There was a lot of hoopla a couple years ago over the intriguing prayer of Jabez in the Bible, and I do love that biblical character's apparent godly ambition. But I find the prayer of Jehoshaphat much more compelling. It's just more relevant to my life! He says, *God, we cannot handle this. But you are in control.*

WHAT YOU DO WITH FEAR

As someone said, the problem is not your fear. Your problem is what you *do* with your fear.

When you feel overwhelmed, do you let that destabilize you, depress you, and discourage you? Or like Jehoshaphat, do you admit your fear and lay it at the feet of the sovereign God?

I like what Rick Warren wrote on a Facebook post: [53]

> Never let an impossible situation intimidate you. Let it motivate you. Let it motivate you to pray more. Let it motivate you to trust more.

After Jehoshaphat prays, the Spirit of the Lord gives a pep talk through one of the guys in the crowd, quite unexpectedly. A man named Jahaziel stands up and says,

> *This is what the* LORD *says: "Do not be afraid! Don't be discouraged by this mighty army, for the battle is not yours, but God's!"* 2 CHRONICLES 20:15 (NLT)

The people are so inspired that they end up putting together a worship service rather than a battle plan. And as it turns out, the three enemy armies end up destroying each other, for reasons that remain a mystery to the Israelites. When all is said and done, they do not have to lift a single weapon in battle!

THE PRAYER OF JEHOSHAPHAT

If you feel outmatched and outnumbered today, do a Jehoshaphat: Remind yourself that *God is bigger*. Say with the king...

> *You alone are the God who is in heaven. You are ruler of all the kingdoms of the earth. You are powerful and mighty; no one can stand against you! Your faithful love endures forever!*

Tomorrow: More stories of how God helped someone surrounded by enemies!

God is… bigger.

QUESTIONS FOR REFLECTION:

What intrigues, inspires, or interests you about 2 Chronicles 20:1–12?

Can you relate to Jehoshaphat? Is there an area in your life where you are afraid and feel overwhelmed?

Is there an area where you hesitate to trust God's sovereignty over your life?

Today pray the prayer of Jehoshaphat!

GOD IS SOVEREIGN
WHEN I'M SURROUNDED

READ YOUR BIBLE: *Psalm 23:5–6*

SPOTLIGHT VERSE: *You prepare a table before me in the presence of my enemies.* PSALM 23:5

IN BILLY GRAHAM'S AUTOBIOGRAPHY *Just As I Am* there are so many great stories of our sovereign God working through the most disheartening events.

Graham writes about his first big campaign in England. He received antagonistic press coverage from the very start. The newspapers decided to rip into Billy Graham, painting him as a lunatic.

They were led by a wildly popular, cynical columnist for a London newspaper whose pen name was Cassandra. He tricked Graham into getting his picture taken in a bar. Although Graham was just drinking apple juice, Cassandra printed the photograph and wrote a caption that made him look like a horrible, sleazy, money-grubbing evangelist lush.

The campaign had reserved an auditorium that would seat 12,000 people for a span of six weeks. After Cassandra's column, one by one all the supporting churches dropped out. They called Graham's office and essentially said, "We can't be associated with this lunatic."

Everything looked bleak. Nothing but embarrassment and financial ruin seemed ahead.

What happened next?

All the controversy kept away the wimpy Christians who didn't want to be seen in the company of someone with a bad reputation and instead brought out all the cynics, all the hard-bitten, hard-hearted people. They were attracted to controversy, and wanted to see Billy Graham fail so they could make fun of him. The possibility of a train wreck will always attract spectators.

On the opening night, the first several rows were filled with press people who showed up at the last minute. The reporters came for a whole week waiting for him to do something flamboyant or crazy.

Then something funny happened. Some of these guys started finding their hearts softened instead.

There were stories like this: A couple of tough, jaded guys were sitting in the back row. One of them said, "I don't want you to think I'm religious; I just showed up to make fun of this guy." The other man said, "Me too."

At the end of the meeting the first guy turned to the second and said, "I don't know about you, but I'm going forward. I want to learn more about Jesus." The other man said, "Me too. By the way, here's your wallet. I'm a pickpocket."

Members of the press started coming to Jesus—and giving Billy Graham unexpected positive publicity! Even though the church people were still staying away, others came to see what the newspapers were writing about. The meetings grew larger and larger.

At the end of six weeks they had to extend the campaign another six weeks.

At the end of three months they had to rent the 122,000-seat Wembley Stadium—the largest stadium in England—for their final night. Then demand grew so large, they decided to rent another soccer stadium that seated 65,000 people right next to it. A total of 187,000 people came out in one night to hear Billy Graham— the largest single religious gathering in the history of England!

After that last night, Winston Churchill phoned Billy Graham and said, "I need to talk to you." Graham came to his house to find Churchill with the three evening newspapers spread out in front of him. He said, "If I and Marilyn Monroe went to Wembley Stadium, we *together* couldn't fill that place. What's going on?"

Billy Graham said, "I'm talking about hope. People need hope in war-torn Britain."

Churchill replied, "I look at these newspapers, and I have no hope for the future."

And Graham answered, "Let me tell you about the hope of Christ."

Churchill let Graham go on; even after Churchill's secretary came in and said, "Sir there's another appointment waiting for you," Churchill said, "Let 'em wait!" [54]

I don't know what Churchill did with what he heard. But to me that whole story is an example of the sovereign God moving in powerful ways.

Billy Graham was slandered and maligned and painted unfairly. But God had a plan to use even *that* to reach people.

And God can do the exact same thing for you.

God is… the One Who brings good out of chaos.

QUESTIONS FOR REFLECTION

What situation in your life right now makes you feel surrounded by enemies, as Billy Graham was in today's story? Pray that God will somehow, in His sovereignty, bring good even out of that—and trust that He will!

Write down a brief, encouraging memory of how God worked in and through a tough situation in your life:

GOD IS SOVEREIGN AND GOD IS GOOD

READ YOUR BIBLE: *Romans 8:28–31*

SPOTLIGHT VERSE: *And we know that in all things God works for the good of those who love him, who have been called according to his purpose.* ROMANS 8:28

TERRY WAS ONE OF the most beautiful women I've ever met.

In a previous book, *Thrill Ride*, I told the story of how I ran into her. I was speaking at a family camp when I first witnessed her enthusiastically greeting people walking into the chapel. Here's what I saw: A young woman with symptoms of very severe cerebral palsy. Both legs and her right arm were tied to her wheelchair—apparently because she could no longer control them. Even her left arm flailed wildly in the air as she said hello to the camp guests.

When I heard Terry speak, I could barely understand her because of the thick cerebral palsy "accent." She'd smile her crooked smile at each person who entered as she said, "G-G-G-G-G-OOD M-M-M-M-ORNING!!! H-H-HOW A-A-A-RE Y-Y-Y-YOU?" Every sentence was laborious for her.

Yet, along with everyone else at the camp, I fell in love with this young woman who radiated a rare joy in Christ.

But then came the talent show. The second-to-last night of camp, anyone who signed up could perform on the auditorium stage. Little kids played piano. A teenager showed off some amazing musical skill on the viola. There was an adorable preschool dance troupe. And finally the emcee introduced the last act:

"Will you please welcome our friend Terry, who will wrap it all up for us with a song!"

And my heart sank. I thought, "Oh, no. Poor Terry. She's just going to embarrass herself and make this a very awkward moment for all of us."

The host continued, "And her talent is… she will lead us in worship!" My heart sank even further. How could Terry, who could barely speak, possibly do this? I say this to my shame, because I was being very shallow.

So Terry was wheeled up on stage. The emcee adjusted a microphone on a boom so it aimed at her mouth. She shouted "OK-K-KAY!!!" to the sound man, who started a musical background track for the tune she was about to sing.

And I could tell from the melody what song it was.

"God is so good."

And I thought, *this?* Of all the songs she could have chosen, *Terry* is singing *this?* I'd always associated this old chorus with a somewhat superficial view of life. How can she possibly sing these lyrics with any enthusiasm after all the hard knocks she's had?

But as the music played, she tilted back her head to heaven, looked up, and as tears streamed down her face she sang with gusto,

"G-G-G-G-G-G-G-OD IS S-S-S-O G-G-G-G-OOD!
G-G-G-G-G-G-G-OD IS S-S-S-O G-G-G-G-OOD!
HE'S S-S-S-O G-G-G-GOOD T-T-TO M-M-M-ME!!!!!!"

And in an instant, everyone who could stand, stood. Those who couldn't stand, lifted hands to heaven, and those who couldn't do that, tilted their faces back like Terry. And also like her, we were all weeping. With pure joy. At the goodness of God.

I've been in a lot of worship services in my life, but never one that rocketed the whole congregation directly into a sense of the presence of God like the one led by Terry. [55]

How could she sing *"God is so good"*? Because she knew an important truth about God.

He is sovereign. But that alone is not necessarily comforting—there have been evil sovereigns. Terry knew: God is good.

God promises her, and you, too, that although you may never see it in this lifetime, He will redeem every one of your trials on earth, and will one day restore you, both physically and spiritually.

Walk through today's key verse with me:

"*We know...*" This is a truth we can cling to with certainty.

"*...God works...*" He's the one who makes it happen. I don't need to worry if I don't have a plan. He's the one who turns it around.

"*...all things...*" Even a divorce? Even an infant death? Even something that was my own stupid mistake? Yes, even that. I'm not saying He caused all of it directly. But I am saying He permits it, and can work through it.

"*...for good... according to His purpose.*" God has a purpose: Romans 8:28 doesn't really make sense without Romans 8:29, which explains that God's plan is to make you like Jesus.

If you really *believe* this—that your loving God is in control—it'll make your confidence soar!

Because there's nothing God can't turn into gold.

No mistake He can't turn into a masterpiece.

No problem He can't turn around and use for good.

In fact, I believe your *greatest ministry* will come from your *greatest pain*. Terry was the most effective worship leader I have ever experienced, and she can barely speak! It was her pain that gave her testimony such credibility.

But how exactly does the Romans 8:28 promise happen, even when everything seems to be going wrong? We'll spend some more time in Romans 8 tomorrow!

God is... sovereign, and God is good.

QUESTIONS FOR REFLECTION

How can there be so much suffering if God truly exists? Some believe there are only two explanations: Either God is not sovereign, or God is not good. How would you respond to that argument?

Give to God your pain and worries and shame now; ask Him to help you trust that He will, by His grace, work together all things, even these things, for good.

GOD'S SOVEREIGNTY
LEADS TO HOPE

READ YOUR BIBLE: *Romans 8:32–39*

SPOTLIGHT VERSE: *Who shall separate us from the love of Christ? Shall trouble or hardship or persecution or famine or nakedness or danger or sword?* ROMANS 8:35

HE THOUGHT HE WAS going to die.

Jeff Miller is a computer salesman who was reading a book on a flight home when there was a muffled thump. The rear engine in the tail of the DC-10 had exploded and the jet was now rudderless; it couldn't be steered anymore. It swayed violently from side to side.

The pilots tried for an emergency landing in Sioux City, Iowa. Some passengers were sobbing. Some were shaking. Some were screaming. They were heading toward a plane crash. And almost certain death.

Can you imagine being in that plane?

You may remember seeing news footage of the plane, cartwheeling on the runway. It exploded in flames.

Miller braced himself for a violent death but it never came. After the spinning landing, he found himself upside down, in a corn field, still strapped in his seat, not a mark on him. Amazing! He was one of a few passengers who miraculously survived.

Lee Strobel, a prize winning Chicago journalist who is now a pastor, interviewed Miller. Most people don't survive a plane crash from 35,000 feet. What did it feel like?

Jeff told him, "I tell you the truth, it was scary, but at the same time I felt like I was full of hope." [56]

Full of hope.

He went on,

> There was hope if I lived; and the hope that if I died I'd be with Christ. Like it says in the Bible, what can anybody do to you if your hope is in the Lord? [57]

Full of hope.

THE CURE FOR HOPELESSNESS

The Bible's all about hope. There are 86 references to hope in the Old Testament. 80 references to hope in the New Testament. Four references to it in Romans 8 alone. You think God wants you to have hope?

Absolutely. Because hopelessness is the biggest source of stress in life. And a rock-solid belief that God is sovereign is the cure.

After church last week a very serious eleven-year old boy approached me. He was so grim for someone his age. I could tell something was really bothering him.

He told me in a surprisingly world-weary tone, "I am really struggling with anxiety. I hear people talking about the future, and the end of the world, and wars and terrorism, and late at night I can't sleep and I worry about all of this and get really scared."

I opened the Bible to the end of Romans 8, and asked him to read me those verses out loud. I could see the stress just rolling off him, his shoulders going from tense to relaxed as he read Paul's inspired words.

And I gave him an assignment: I put together a list of verses about God's sovereignty, and asked him to write those verses out onto 3×5 cards and read them several times a day for an entire week. He got it: "So I can replace my anxious thoughts with the truth?" "That's exactly right!" I said.

GREATER THAN ANY POWER

In Romans 8, Paul gives a list that sounds like the ingredients for a nightmare: Death, angels, demons, the future… yet, he proclaims, not one of these powers can ever separate us from God's loving plan.

This does not mean life is smooth all of the time.

But even if things look bleak; even if, as Paul puts it, "we are like lambs to be slaughtered" (which certainly was the experience of many first-century persecuted Christians, and many today); even in those circumstances, God's sovereign love ultimately holds me tight and brings me home to Him.

Day 42: God's Sovereignty Leads to Hope

DO I NEED TO THINK ABOUT SOVEREIGNTY?

I'll admit it: Because God's sovereignty is so *other*, so outside of my ability to comprehend, at times I feel like a puppy, head cocked to one side, trying desperately to understand what my Master is trying to say.

That doesn't mean the Master's voice is spouting nonsense. It means I'm encountering Someone different than me.

Remember, the Bible is describing a Being who is not just a bigger version of you, ruling a bigger version of a human kingdom; it's describing a reality far beyond your comprehension. The Roman or Norse gods are a lot easier to understand. But they're not real.

In the end, when I consider the sovereignty of God, I must concede that if there is a God, He is simply not possible for me to fully understand.

So why did God even mention some of these hard-to-understand attributes, like sovereignty? Why not just leave them for us to appreciate in heaven, when we can comprehend these mysteries better?

God wanted to reveal the truth of His sovereignty to you and me for a reason:

It makes a difference in your life now.

It means you can let go of your revenge fantasies.

It means there is a place to put your fears.

It means you can sleep better tonight.

A suggestion: Do what that eleven-year old did.

Put some of the key verses from the daily readings in this book onto index cards, and carry them around with you every day for the rest of this study, starting today. Read them when you wake up, when you go to bed, and perhaps at lunchtime or during breaks.

If you believe He is ultimately in control, what is there to fear?

Nothing.

God is... the One who gives hope.

QUESTIONS FOR REFLECTION

Of Paul's list of scary things in Romans 8:35, which scares you the most?

How does a belief in God's sovereignty build hope and reduce fear?

What practical, emotional benefits do you see to a faith in a God who is sovereign over all?

WEEK 7

GOD IS

Immutable
Worthy of Worship

This thought brings comfort as we enter into the perplexities of each day: amid all the changes and uncertainties of life, God and His Christ remain the same — almighty to save. J. I. PACKER

DAY 43
GOD NEVER CHANGES

READ YOUR BIBLE: *Psalm 36*

SPOTLIGHT VERSE: *Your love, Lord, reaches to the heavens, your faithfulness to the skies.* PSALM 36:5

EVER WORRY ABOUT WHETHER you're going to heaven? Wonder if you are "still saved"?

When we first moved to Santa Cruz, my daughter Elisabeth was just eighteen months old. We took her one day to a beachside amusement park, and rode on the Sky Ride, which is something like a chair lift: You sit on a bench which hangs from a cable 20 or 30 feet in the air as you glide over the park, your legs dangling.

And right after we reached the middle of the ride, Elisabeth started freaking out.

She was one car behind me with my wife Laurie, and as I looked back to find out why Elisabeth was screaming I saw her squirm away from Laurie, trying to get out of the gondola, slipping under the safety bar...

218

Day 43: *God Never Changes*

Laurie says she's never felt an adrenaline rush like that before! She grabbed Elisabeth and held on for dear life—Elisabeth's life! As I watched helplessly, Elisabeth pushed Laurie away, letting go of her several times. Her sandals came off and spiraled to the sand 30 feet below.

But Laurie never let go of Elisabeth. I watched my wife in true mama-bear mode, straining with all her might to prevent that child from slipping away. Why? Well, because my wife loves her daughter! Fiercely!

There are times in your life when you squirm and twist and want to get away from God. And you may in fact let go of Him. *But God does not let go of you.* Why? Because He loves you. Fiercely.

Jesus said of His followers:

> *"I give them eternal life, and they will never perish. No one can snatch them away from me, for my Father has given them to me, and he is more powerful than anyone else. No one can snatch them from the Father's hand."* JOHN 10:28–29 (NLT)

God's faithfulness to you is just one implication of the unchanging nature of God.

GOD IS ROCK SOLID

Theologians refer to this as *immutability* of God. This means He is unchangeable, consistent, rock solid, always reliable. What He was, He always will be. He *never* changes.

219

Everything else I see in my world changes. My house needs paint. My car is rusting. I'm aging. Even the 2,000-year-old redwood trees in the hills near my house change.

Everything changes. *Except God.*

I used to wonder—how can that be true? After all, God is not inactive; God did create the universe. The Word did become flesh. So doesn't that mean God changes?

Of course, God is *active*. God *responds*. God *creates*. In that sense God *does* change because He changes His *activity*. (Or I should say, *from our perspective* He changes His activity. If God is outside of time and space, then He is "always active and always at rest", as Augustine pointed out).

But immutability means God's *attributes* don't change. God's *character* doesn't change. He will *always be* all the things we have seen in this study:

> *Whatever is good and perfect comes down to us from God our Father, who created all the lights in the heavens.* **He never changes** *or casts a shifting shadow.* JAMES 1:17 (NLT)

> *He who is the Glory of Israel does not lie or change his mind; for* **he is not a human being, that he should change his mind.** 1 SAMUEL 15:29

> *Jesus Christ is* **the same yesterday and today and forever.** HEBREWS 13:8

Day 43: God Never Changes

GOD IS FAITHFUL

It's one of the most *"other"* attributes of God: *He never changes!*

What else can you really count on in life to *never* change?

You can't count on your employer. Companies get bought, and workers laid off, all the time.

You can't count on your stock portfolio.

You can't count on the government.

You can't count on the economy.

You can't count on the weather.

Maybe other people have proven to you just how changeable human loyalties can be. Someone said "I love you." Then changed their mind. Someone promised you forever. But didn't mean it.

Know this:

> *God is not a man, that he should lie, nor a son of man, that he should change his mind. Does he speak and then not act? Does he promise and not fulfill?*
> NUMBERS 23:19 (NIV, 1984)

> *The LORD is trustworthy in all he promises and faithful in all he does.* PSALM 145:13B

Note that phrase: *"Trustworthy in all He promises."* There are over 7,000 promises in the Bible. God is faithful and trustworthy to fulfill them *all*. Like this:

He will keep you strong to the end so that you will be free from all blame on the day when our Lord Jesus Christ returns. **God will do this, for he is faithful** to *do what he says...* 1 CORINTHIANS 1:8–9A (NLT)

Next time you feel insecure in your standing with God, remind yourself: God is faithful to all His promises, including His promise to save those who trust in Him. He will never let you go.

God is... immutable.

QUESTIONS TO PONDER:

In what way are you struggling with feeling insecure in your relationship with God?

What difference does it make to you to believe God is totally reliable, faithful, steady, and unchangeable?

THE LORD WILL PROVIDE

READ YOUR BIBLE: *Psalm 100*

SPOTLIGHT VERSE: *For the LORD is good and his love endures forever; his faithfulness continues through all generations.* PSALM 100:5

AFTER MY DAD DIED, our family lived beneath the poverty line for about eight years. Many times my single mother said to my little sister and me in her heavily Swiss-German accented English, "Ve haff no money for food! Ve must pray!"

I remember holding hands in our kitchen, a little circle of three, asking God, quite literally, for our daily bread. And God always provided—though not always in the way I would have preferred.

For instance, once we specifically asked for milk, and the very next morning we found a box of powdered milk on our doorstep. *Which I couldn't stand.* But it did provide what we needed. To this day I have no idea how it got there, or who donated it.

Another day we asked for shoes, and the next day shoes just my size were left in a bag on the porch—and they were the ugliest puke-green shoes I have ever seen in my life. I told Mom, "There is no way I am wearing those to school!" And she explained to me in her patient, logical way, "YOU VILL WEAR ZEM!!!"

So I did. And everyone at school thought they were so cool—the one and only time they ever thought that of me at school!

But incidents like that made an impression on me.

Recently I was preparing to speak at the funeral of a man who died at about the same age as my father, leaving two young children and a widow, just like our family, many years ago. I asked my mother what words of wisdom she had for this woman who was about to walk the same path she had walked.

She stopped and thought for a moment and then said one phrase. Four words.

"The Lord will provide."

Talk about an antidote to discouragement.

"The Lord will provide." She told me, "I've seen it again and again." And then together we remembered more of the ways God literally put food on our table.

Day 44: The Lord Will Provide

GOD IS FAITHFUL TO PROVIDE

Here's a verse that was written by the Apostle Paul after he'd been in prison, beaten for his faith, shipwrecked, sick, homeless, laughed at, slandered, taken to court... whatever you can go through in life, he'd been there. And he says, guess what I've learned?

> *And my God will meet all your needs according to his glorious riches in Christ Jesus.* PHILIPPIANS 4:19

The Lord will provide.

I love the true story of George Müller. He was a remarkable man who lived in the 1800s.

By his own admission he was a rotten kid. Started stealing at age 10... from his own family! Ended up in prison, an alcoholic.

But then he totally changed. Became a Christian. And decided God was calling him to reach out to kids just like him.

He started Christian homes for London's street children. This was way before his time. No one in the world was doing this then. He ended up housing 10,000 street kids, mostly orphans, in his homes.

Think of how stressed you get making ends meet for yourself, or for a family of two or three kids. He had *thousands* of kids to worry about.

But the really amazing thing is this: He never asked for funds. Not one time. He said it was a grand experiment to see if God really was faithful. I don't recommend this for everyone, but it sure worked out for George Müller. Not one child ever went without a meal. Not one person ever had to settle for an I.O.U.

George Müller's favorite saying: *"God is faithful still and hears prayers still!"*

The Lord will provide.

GREAT IS GOD'S FAITHFULNESS

There will be dark times in all of our lives. You may be in a dark time right now. But I love the saying:

"Never doubt in the dark what God has taught you in the light."

In the past few weeks you've learned about God's holiness, love, omnipotence, omniscience, omnipresence, sovereignty…

And now know this: None of that will ever change.

God is the same yesterday, today, and forever. (SEE HEBREWS 13:8)

Those truths about Him never shift, no matter what you are going through! Cling to them. Focus on them, instead of the problems around you.

The grayer I get, the more I sing *"Great Is Thy Faithfulness"* with gusto. Because I have more and more memories of God's provision. I know this: The Lord will provide!

God is… faithful.

QUESTIONS TO PONDER:

What specific situations or memories in your life reinforce God's immutability and faithfulness?

Write a brief statement specifically about immutability and what it means to you: "Because God never changes…"

GOD NEVER CHANGES, BUT WHAT I BELIEVE CHANGES ME

READ YOUR BIBLE: *Psalm 46*

SPOTLIGHT VERSE: *God is our refuge and strength, an ever-present help in trouble. Therefore we will not fear...*
PSALM 46:1–2A

I STARTED THIS STUDY by stating that how you define God changes everything about how you respond to life.

So consider these differing definitions of God:

"The eternal mind"—Plato

"God is the absolute Spirit, yet a spirit without consciousness until it becomes conscious in the reason and the thoughts of man."—Hegel

"Pure mathematical mind..."—Einstein

"The ground of all being."—Aristotle

As brilliant as they all were, these men were all attempting to define God, to pin Him down. And again, being humans, they tend to fashion a god in their own image. Is it any surprise to you that Plato the philosopher defines God as a "mind," or Einstein the mathematician describes God as "mathematical"?

Meanwhile the Bible speaks of God as beyond imagining—and yet knowable! It describes Him in all the ways we've seen and more: "God is... Love... All-Powerful... All-Knowing... Always Present... Sovereign... Faithful... Unchanging...."

THE DIFFERENCE THIS MAKES

Okay, now imagine yourself in various life situations.

You're alone on a business trip tempted to compromise your integrity.

You've been rejected by someone you love.

You're facing the death of a loved one.

How would the various definitions above change the way you handle each situation?

Try praying, "The Lord is my eternal mind, I shall not want..." Just not quite the same inspirational ring as the familiar verse in Psalm 23, is it?

In today's verses the Psalmist declares that *because* he believes the Lord to be a refuge, to be strong, *"**therefore we will not fear.**"*

Day 45: ...But What I Believe Changes Me

What he believed about God changed his response to his crisis. And what you believe to be true about God really changes you too — down to the core of your being. When you really believe God is as powerful, as present, as full of pardon as you've seen in this study, you will be changed — forever!

PRACTICAL AND POWERFUL PRAYERS

I recently went on a trip to Mexico with my son's 7th grade class to work in an orphanage there. One evening we went to a very poor Tecate neighborhood built next to a sewage treatment plant. The smell of human waste permeated the place, so intense that my eyes stung.

But then we joined with a local church's midweek service. This church burned no incense, but their intense and authentic worship of God quickly overpowered all other distractions. I was caught up in the fresh enthusiasm of it all! It was so inspiring to hear praise songs I knew in English sung in another language. I enjoyed listening to the sermon, even though I speak absolutely no Spanish. I loved how the pastor ended the message with an altar call, a time for people to come forward for prayer. In fact, I felt like I was just glowing with joy through the entire experience — until one of the pastors asked me to walk up and pray with people during the altar call — and I went pale!

"But!" I objected, "I don't speak the language!"

"Is okay! Is okay!" the pastor smiled as she took me by the arm to the front of the church, gesturing toward crying people who needed prayer.

Day 45: ...But What I Believe Changes Me

So I walked up nervously, put my arms around people who whispered their stories, and thought: "What can I possibly pray that is relevant to their situations, since I can't understand what they were saying?"

Then I prayed, in English, "God... you are omniscient, and that means you are multilingual! And you know this need better than I could ever hope to know it—even if I spoke the language! You are omnipresent. That means You're right here with us now, crossing every border. You're omnipotent. That means You have the power to meet this need. You are faithful and sovereign, so You know exactly the right course of action for this situation. You are love. That means You love this person so much. And we both love You. So we lift this need to You now in full assurance that You know and You care and You will work."

I was able to pray again and again with power and with passion as the altar call continued. Those who clearly needed further guidance I steered toward Spanish speakers after the service ended. But through that experience I learned firsthand just how an appreciation of God's attributes can help as life throws you unexpected challenges.

PRAYING THE ATTRIBUTES

Try *praying* through the attributes of God you've learned in the last seven weeks. Notice how it makes an immediate impact to affirm these truths. Actually address God and pray through these next sentences:

*You are the **omnipotent** God.*

You are bigger than any problem. Nothing is too difficult for You. And I can do all things through You.

Day 45: ...But What I Believe Changes Me

*You are the **omniscient** God.*

You know all things. You know my needs. You know my challenges. You know the needs of those around me.

*You are the **omnipresent** God.*

You are right here, right now. With me. With my loved ones. The Lord is in this place. And I know it.

*You are the **sovereign** God.*

You are in control. You guarantee that all things work together for good for those called according to Your purpose.

*You are **love**.*

As infinitely powerful as You are, God, You are just as loving. The matchless power that it took to make the universe is matched by the power of love You have for me, and for my loved ones, and for my enemies. Help me to love them all as You love them. You loved us all so much that you came to this earth to make a way to You.

*You are **immutable** and **faithful**.*

You never change. You will keep every promise You have made. You are faithful to keep me secure in Your salvation. You are faithful to provide. You are faithful to reward.

Thank you, God, for these glimpses into the amazing reality that is far beyond any earthly imagination! Help my mind to reel, my soul to be comforted, my heart to soar as I think of your wonders!

When I consider the infinite nature of all these attributes, Lord, I realize anew:

God is... enough!

QUESTIONS TO PONDER:

What difference do you think it would make if you strengthened your understanding of the "enoughness" of God? What difference has it made?

Do you know anyone who needs to have their faith in such a God strengthened? How can you help?

DAY 46
CHRISTIAN ATHEISTS

READ YOUR BIBLE: *Isaiah 29:13,14*

SPOTLIGHT VERSE: *They claim to know God, but by their actions they deny him.* TITUS 1:16A

THERE'S A DANGER IN Christianity today, a little different than what I called "pagan Christians" earlier. It's a danger you could fall into after this study. A danger I need to warn you about.

Christian atheism.

Craig Groeschel is a pastor who wrote a book called *Christian Atheist*. He starts by talking about a time he was on a flight that had two segments.

On the first leg of the flight, he was sitting next to a guy named Travis who asked him what he did for a living, and when Craig replied that he was a pastor, Travis immediately responded, "Oh, I don't believe in God." And went on to defend his atheism.

Day 46: Christian Atheists

When the plane landed at the first stop, Travis got off and a young woman named Michelle took his place. She instantly started talking about everything she was anxious about in her life— how she felt nervous about flying, was having problems with a boyfriend she lived with, felt upset about her finances.

Then when she asked Craig what he did for a living, and he said, "I'm a pastor," Michelle exclaimed, "I believe in God too!" In fact, she said, she had received Jesus a long time ago. But then she broke down in tears and admitted, "I believe in God, but I know my life doesn't look like what a Christian's life is supposed to look like."

Craig says he was struck in that moment by the realization that there's more than one kind of atheist:

There's the traditional, philosophical atheist, who does not believe in God at all, like Travis.

But then there's the *Christian atheist*. Like Michelle. And maybe like you and me, at times. [58]

I can say I believe in God, and yet for all practical purposes *live* as if the God I say I believe in *does not exist*.

AM I A PRACTICAL ATHEIST?

Ask yourself: *Does my life look like I am a person who believes in the God of the Bible?*

My biggest fear is that you will have merely learned terminology in this study: That your mind has been filled with facts, but those facts haven't trickled down the 12 inches from your brain to your heart.

Day 46: Christian Atheists

We've been studying God's omnipotence, omnipresence, immutability, graciousness, sovereignty, grace...

Do most Christians believe these things are true of God? Maybe theoretically.

But how would you finish this sentence: "I believe in God, but..."

"I believe in God, but I worry all the time."

"I believe in God, but I constantly feel lonely and abandoned."

"I believe in God, but I'm burned out spiritually."

"I believe in God but I have continual anxiety about the future."

"I believe in God but I figure I can live my life however I want to."

I think these are all signs of *Christian atheism*.

They claim to know God, but by their actions they deny him.

I'm not suggesting you'll never have *times* when you feel lonely or anxious—that's just part of the human experience (and those are all emotions even Christ felt at times) —but the *core* of your being can be peaceful, serene, and confident when what the Bible says about God is truly internalized.

ACHIEVEMENT OR ASTONISHMENT

Don't get me wrong: I'm not saying you must *try harder* to internalize these truths. I'm asking if you are beholding the wonders of God so that *your imagination is captured* and you are changed. I'm not talking about *achievement*. I'm talking about *astonishment*.

In today's reading from Isaiah 29, the Lord says that His cure for the practical atheism of the people is this:

> *"I will astound these people with wonder upon wonder."* ISAIAH 29:14

Their hearts have grown stale—and so He will let them witness the wonder of the rocket blast-off!

I pray that the same thing has happened with you as you've studied God's attributes in nature and Scripture.

I pray that you haven't just studied, but that God has put Himself on display and blown you away.

I pray that these amazing truths make a difference in you.

I pray that you keep your eyes wide open for traces of God all around you.

And I pray that if you feel yourself drifting from God in the future you don't try harder to "feel" Him again through the addition of rigorous rules or disciplines. That ways lies spiritual dryness, and a bondage to a kind of legalism.

GOD WITHOUT ADDITIVES

God observes in Isaiah 29 one result of not really knowing Him: Adding human religious rules to worship. *"Their worship of me is based on merely human rules…"*

The people were essentially building an idol.

Not a *statue*. But a *system*.

This is exactly what happens to me, too, when I don't pay attention to what the Bible really says about the identity of God: I complicate and trivialize my faith with all sorts of extra teachings and rules.

Margaret Feinberg, in her book *The Organic God*, uses a food analogy to explain this. As she puts it, the real God of the Bible is *organic*, while the false god we often concoct is a result of putting too many religious additives, preservatives, flavorings, and colorings into the mix. [59]

The solution: Getting back to the 100% natural God. Relaxing, and letting God once again capture your imagination. And all the rest of you too!

I pray that you gaze in wonder at the Father, Son, and Holy Spirit and live in gratitude for God's grace to you in every moment of every day.

May you enjoy the richness of the organic God for the rest of your life!

QUESTIONS TO PONDER:

Does your life look like you are a person who believes in the God of the Bible?

Which attribute of God do you struggle with the most? Why?

DEAR GOD: COUNT ME IN

READ YOUR BIBLE: *1 John 3:1–3*

SPOTLIGHT VERSE: *See what great love the Father has lavished on us, that we should be called children of God! And that is what we are!* 1 JOHN 3:1

EARLIER I QUOTED FROM the book *Children's Letters to God*. I can't get enough of the innocence and honesty in these letters, so here are some more:

> Dear God, If you give me the genie lamp like in Aladdin I will give you anything you want. Except for my chess set. And my money.

> Dear God: Thank you for my baby brother. But what I prayed for was a puppy. [60]

These letters are all cute, but it's striking to me how many times these letters show kids trying to strike the same bargains with God that grown-ups do.

Day 47: Dear God: Count Me In

Often these letters show the kids' thinking of religion as a *quid pro quo* arrangement. That's a Latin phrase meaning "this for that." They reason that if they do certain things, then God will be more or less obligated to give them certain things.

It's like this child's letter to God:

> Dear God: Well I did what I promised but You did not send me the horse yet. What about it?!

Ever do that?

"Well, God, I did not miss a church service all year. But You did not send me the new job yet. What about it?!"

"Well, I went on the mission trip, but You did not send me the new spouse yet. What about it?!"

GOD OWES YOU NOTHING

Jerry Bridges, an author famous for writing about the spiritual disciplines, gives an urgent warning:

> My spiritual disciplines, like a quiet time, Bible study, Scripture memory... formed the foundation for my spiritual growth. However, I came to believe that my day-to-day relationship with God depended on how faithfully I performed them. My experience is not unusual. One student told a friend of mine that he was diligent in his daily quiet time "so that nothing bad will happen to me." [61]

But the Bible says that God is no man's debtor. He is *God*. He does not owe you or me anything! (SEE ROMANS 11:35)

Day 47: Dear God: Count Me In

The more I study the attributes of God, the more I realize: God owes me *nothing*.

He doesn't owe me any answers to prayer.

He doesn't owe me any explanations.

He doesn't owe me a certain quality of life.

I can never do *anything* to put God in my debt, because He is God! If God is God, then He is under no obligation to puny creatures like me.

Yet... God is gracious and loving. He doesn't owe me the blessing of eternal life, but instead *offers* it freely. In fact, He *lavishes* love on me and you.

He designed, He initiated, and He completed the plan for your salvation. There's nothing you can do. So He did it all.

That frees you and me to just receive it.

Like the little boy in this letter:

Dear God: Count me in. Your friend, Herbie.

That's what it looks like to lean fully on the love and grace of God. You don't insist on anything. But you receive everything.

But to all who believed Him and accepted Him, He gave the right to become children of God. JOHN 1:12 (NLT)

We have all benefitted from the rich blessings He brought to us — one gracious blessing after another. JOHN 1:16 (NLT)

Day 47: Dear God: Count Me In

You know what? Being loved like that changes you.

When you're loved lavishly, it changes *everything*.

Everything good I do
is a result of the gratitude I feel
as a recipient of God's grace.

Like Isaiah after he is cleansed, I want to go out for God.
I want to love
and give
and have compassion
and forgive,
because that's what's been done for me!

I pray that you always keep the simple child-like faith of Herbie: Live in simple, awestruck wonder of what God has done out of His infinite love for you!

God is... gracious!

QUESTIONS TO PONDER:

How do you slip into *quid pro quo* thinking? Why are we often tempted to think like that?

Is it difficult for you to think of God as totally gracious? Why or why not?

AWE-FULL WORSHIP

READ YOUR BIBLE: *Isaiah 40:27–31*

SPOTLIGHT VERSE: *Therefore, since we are receiving a kingdom that cannot be shaken, let us be thankful, and so worship God acceptably with reverence and awe.*
HEBREWS 12:28

TWO WORDS THAT SHOULD always be seen as a contradiction: *Boring worship.*

Yet that's exactly how many people see church. In Mark Twain's classic *Tom Sawyer*, Tom goes to church at the demand of his Aunt Polly.

The boring announcements are made from a "list that would stretch out to the crack of doom." The prayer is "generous" in its details. Tom "did not enjoy it but only endured it—if he did that much." The only thing in the whole service that holds his attention is a fly that lands in front of him, to which Tom is hypnotically drawn, taking in every detail, finding the pest far more compelling than the preacher. The sermon, meanwhile, "droned along monotonously through an argument that was so prosy that many a head by and by began to nod." [62]

In a word? Boring.

WIDE WORLD OF WORSHIP

Here's a contrast to that image of church:

I recently returned from speaking at a conference for missionaries in Africa. The first morning, everyone gathered for a time of worship. Picture it: In this one room, there were missionaries there from literally all around the globe. Many different ethnic groups, a variety of languages.

And they were from every Christian denomination you could possibly imagine. Pentecostal. Anglican. Mennonite. Presbyterian. Baptist. They were all there.

This shows just how shallow I can be, but at first I was reminded not of worship, but of that old series of jokes:

How many **Presbyterians** *does it take to change a light bulb?* None. The lights will go on and off at predestined times.

How many **Lutherans** *does it take to change a light bulb?* None. Lutherans don't believe in change.

How many **Unitarians** *does it take to change a light bulb?* We refuse to take a stand for or against light bulbs, but if, in your own journey, you have found that light bulbs work for you, you are invited to write a poem or compose a modern dance, and present it next month at our annual Light Bulb Sunday Service, in which we will explore a number of light bulb traditions, including incandescent, fluorescent, three-way, long-life and tinted, all of which are equally valid paths to luminescence.

And finally...

*How many **Baptists** does it take to change a light bulb?* Baptists don't change light bulbs because then they'd have to raise their hands.

But the thing is, I saw almost *all* these denominations there at the conference in Uganda.

And then the worship starts. And I'm thinking—how's *this* going to work? And here's what I see: In the first row are the Pentecostals who—as soon as the first note of the song is played—instantly are lifting up their hands like they're getting mugged: "WE SURRENDER, LORD!"

And next to them, the Mennonites. Hair up in buns, long dresses—and those were the *men.* Just kidding.

Next to them, there was a Korean charismatic, who was totally into it, weeping as he worshipped, speaking out loud in Korean. The Pentecostals were trying to interpret. (Kidding again.)

And next to him: the Scottish Presbyterians, who describe *themselves* as "The Frozen Chosen." And they say that with *pride!* They were squinting up at the lyrics on the screen. Not singing, as far as I could see. But I could tell by their faces that inside they were saying—(read this with a Scot accent) "Wi' *arrrr* singin'. In arrrrr hearrrts."

Next to them the African Anglicans. Which was a fascinating combination I had never before witnessed.

And you know what? It was *awesome*.

All these groups together, all these different ethnic backgrounds, denominations, languages — worshiping together! All in their different styles, all happy just to be together for a time of refocus and relaxation in God's grace at this conference in Uganda.

That is a foretaste of *heaven!* Look how the Apostle John describes it:

> *After this I looked and there before me was a great multitude that no one could count, from every nation, tribe, people and language, standing before the throne...* REVELATION 7:9A

What a blow to racism! That's a *God's-eye view* of the church worshipping Him. That could never be boring.

WORSHIP IS NOT A SPECTATOR SPORT

Bible scholar Ben Witherington writes,

> Worship is the signal act of Christianity pointing the world not merely toward God, but towards the practice of praising, petitioning, adoring, thanking, serving God. ...What has happened in post-modern Protestant worship is that too often it has been turned into a performance of the few for the many in the pew. But worship is not meant to be a spectator sport like football. It is meant to be a participa-

tory event in which we all get caught up in love and wonder and praise of our God. [63]

I agree. But how does worship become like that? Not by a preacher's nagging.

Worship becomes vital precisely when I focus on God and not myself.

When I dwell on His majesty.

When I'm lost in Him:

> In His power, in His presence,
> in His love, His knowledge,
> His sovereignty, His faithfulness.

Like the writer of today's Bible reading reminds a disenchanted and bored people,

> *Do you not know? Have you not heard? The* LORD *is the everlasting God, the Creator of the ends of the earth.* ISAIAH 40:28

My worship is revitalized when I think of God, not me. When I think of who God is, not how I'm singing, or whether my hands should be up or down, or what others are doing.

I've found that then, even the most "boring" traditional church liturgy, or the most showy, laser-light contemporary service, can be a transforming experience of communal worship. It's when I'm aware of the majesty of God that I stand on tiptoe, or sit on seat-edge, expectant, aware of His presence, humble, open to His working.

I like what Annie Dillard said years ago about worship services in her book *Teaching a Stone to Talk*:

> Does anyone have the foggiest idea what sort of power we so blithely invoke? Or, as I suspect, does no one believe a word of it? The churches are children playing on the floor with their chemistry sets, mixing up a batch of TNT to kill a Sunday morning. It is madness to wear ladies' straw hats and velvet hats to church; we should all be wearing crash helmets. [64]

What sort of power do you invoke?

God is... worthy of worship!

QUESTION TO PONDER:
What has been your most meaningful and moving worship experience? What made it so?

ENJOYING GOD

READ YOUR BIBLE: *Psalm 34:1–10*

SPOTLIGHT VERSE: *Taste and see that the Lord is good.
Oh, the joys of those who trust in Him!* PSALM 34:8 (NLT)

BLAISE PASCAL WAS ONE of the greatest geniuses in human history.

At 12, he was working out geometry problems that had never been solved.

In his mid-20s he invented a mechanical calculator.

He did ground-breaking research on atmospheric pressure and vacuums.

He also did the foundational work on theories of probability.

And did I mention he lived in the 1600s? And he did all this before his death at age 39? He must have seemed like a man from the future.

Like many people he slowly found himself falling away from his childhood Christianity. Then he found his interest in that faith slowly rekindled. He decided to pick up the Gospels and read them again.

And on the evening of November 23, 1654, he had what he called a "definite conversion." It was a sudden, unexpected, overwhelming experience of the majesty of God.

I love how poetically he describes this mysterious, ecstatic experience in his journal from that night:

> From about half past ten at night until about half past midnight,
>
> FIRE.
>
> GOD of Abraham, GOD of Isaac, GOD of Jacob
> not of the philosophers and of the learned.
> Certitude. Certitude. Feeling. Joy. Peace.
> GOD of Jesus Christ
> My God and your God
> Your GOD will be my God
> Forgetfulness of the world and of everything, except GOD.
> He is only found by the ways taught in the Gospel...
> Joy, joy, joy, tears of joy...
> This is eternal life, that they know you, the one true God, and the one that you sent, Jesus Christ.
> Jesus Christ. Jesus Christ.
> I left Him; I fled Him, renounced, crucified.
> Let me never be separated from Him...
> Renunciation, total and sweet.
> Complete submission to Jesus Christ... [65]

This intellectual genius met God. Or as he wrote, GOD.

And when you meet GOD, not some godlet you fashion, there is a point when His love and His majesty

 ignites you

  and zooms you

   right past the atmosphere of the self

    and into the infinite cosmos of pure worship.

Joy, joy, joy, tears of joy…

BRUSHES WITH GOD

When I read Pascal's description of his conversion I'm moved to tears. Because it helps me remember. My soul too has brushed up against GOD in unexpected moments.

I've had to pull over my car, so saturated with a sense of GOD I could no longer drive. I've casually glanced out my window at the neighborhood when suddenly an awareness of divine love for what I was seeing seemed to cascade through me—like I was caught beneath a waterfall of God's wonderful passion. More frequently I've found myself deeply moved during congregational worship, giving myself to God again with tears of joy and awe.

 Certitude. Certitude. Feeling. Joy. Peace.

WHY I'M HERE

A heart filled with joy and love is one of the effects of trust in God:

Day 49: Enjoying God

For we know how dearly God loves us, because he has given us the Holy Spirit to fill our hearts with his love. ROMANS 5:5B (NLT)

Those who look to Him for help will be radiant with joy... PSALM 34:5 (NLT)

I will be filled with joy because of you; I will sing praises to your name, O Most High. PSALM 9:2 (NLT)

Of course emotions can become idols, too, and I should never serve God just because I get emotions out of the deal. But...

But *enjoying* God is what I am *made* for.

As the Westminster Catechism affirms, "the chief end of man is to *glorify* God and *enjoy* Him forever."

I remember when I first read that as a kid I thought someone was playing a joke on me. *Enjoy* God? It seemed almost irreverent. No, I thought: My job is to *work hard* for God. Not to enjoy Him!

Wrong.

The chief end of man really is to *glorify* God and *enjoy* Him forever.

So how do you *glorify* a Being that already has all glory?

It's what we've been doing in this study. You *notice* His glories. You *thank* Him for His glories. And you *share* with others the glories of God you've been discovering.

As you *glorify* God, you grow to *enjoy* God, to lose yourself in His majesty and grace.

"In commanding us to glorify Him, God is inviting us to enjoy Him." —C.S. Lewis [66]

I hope you've found that your enjoyment of God has been growing. It's a foretaste of heaven, because there you will be in bliss, enjoying God forever.

As the ancient church leader St. Augustine wrote in his *Confessions*:

> Great are you, O Lord, and exceedingly worthy of praise; your power is immense, and your wisdom beyond reckoning. And so we creatures, who are a part of your creation, long to praise you …because you have made us and drawn us to yourself, and our heart is restless until it rests in you. [67]

How does that move you?

God is… the One I was made to enjoy forever.

QUESTIONS TO PONDER:

Can you relate to Blaise Pascal's experience? How so?

How has your enjoyment of God grown through this study?

MORE GOD MOMENTS AHEAD

READ YOUR BIBLE: *Psalm 8*

SPOTLIGHT VERSE: *Lord, our Lord, how majestic is your name in all the earth!* PSALM 8:9

YOU MADE IT! I pray that 50 days of keeping your eyes open to the wonders of God has begun or deepened a lifelong habit for you.

In fact I hope your life is filled with God-moments: Moments when you're rushing to an appointment, or braving the weekday commute, or walking out to get the paper...

...and you see
the sunrise
a sparrow
the stars

And you think: Wow. God made that. And God made me. *And loves me!*

About three thousand years ago someone else had one of those moments. A young shepherd was busy herding his father's flocks. Probably thinking of shearing them and moving them to better pasture and watching for predators.

And then night fell. And he looked up at the stars.

And he said to himself: Wow. And he wrote:

> O LORD, our Lord, how majestic is Your name in all the earth! You have set your glory above the heavens. PSALM 8:1

David was having a sense of God as *Wholly Other*.

God, You are not like the other so-called gods: Gods of a family clan or of the land or of the sea. You are above *all* that. Yet… you reveal yourself to the smallest of us.

GOD AND THE KIDS

> From the lips of children and infants you have ordained praise because of your enemies, to silence the foe and the avenger. PSALM 8:2

I've quoted several of those *Children's Letters to God* so why not a couple more? I love the way these kids have a sense of wonder:

> Dear God, are you as big as the whole sky and as strong as the whole world? That's a good thing. Very much, Dean.

> Oh Lord, thank you for giving me my dad and mother. And their children. And dog and fish. Thank you for giving us the nice world to live in. And eyes

to see it. And what we eat and brains to think. Thank you for ever-thing. Love, Maxine. [68]

That could be a psalm right there. Can **you** be that thankful?

Then David's gaze moves from kids to the cosmos.

GOD AND THE COSMOS

When I consider your heavens, the work of your fingers, the moon and the stars, which you have set in place... PSALM 8:3

Like we've done in this book, David considers the heavens. And he says as amazing as they are, they're *"the work of your fingers."*

The famous Bible translator (and my friend) Ron Allen told me the Hebrew word used there means *"finger-play."* To explain the concept, Ron asked me if I remembered Rosey Grier.

"Of course!" I said "The amazing football player!"

Then Ron said, "Do you remember his hobby? It was needlepoint!" And it all came back to me: How, even during interviews, this muscle-bound NFL star would be working on dainty sewing projects. Ron explained, "That's the image here. To the mighty, powerful God, the whole heavens are like a finger-craft."

WHO AM I?

But David says when he thinks of all this, he asks,

> ...*what is man that you are mindful of him, the son of man that you care for him?* PSALM 8:4

Maybe after this 50-day meditation on the attributes of God you too ask, "Who am I, that God should be mindful of me?"

"I have a bad past."
"I am not very religious."
"I have made so many mistakes."
"Who am I that He should be mindful of *me?*"

I hope during this study you've learned why God cares. It's not because of your religiosity or good deeds. It's because, as I've emphasized, God is *perfect in love.*

God's power is amazing. God's knowledge and sovereignty and omnipresence too. But of all His wonders, there's one that's most amazing:

His love for you and me.

When I realize that, like David, I have to conclude:

> O LORD, *our Lord, how majestic is Your name in all the earth!* PSALM 8:9

May you be *"filled to the measure of all the fullness of God"* (EPHESIANS 3:19) all the days of your life.

PRAYER

Lord, thank you so much for Your love. I pray that all of us who have walked through this study would have an experience of worship that comes from the contrast:

God, You are so big. Yet—You choose to call my name and find me and save me. And hold me. May I live in awe of You today and surrender to Your love as You hold me.

EXTRAS FOR:

GOD IS

Articles:
"Is God Male?"
"Is Belief in God Harmful?"

Music Playlist
Literary Resources
Memory Verses

Small Group Lessons

IS GOD MALE?

IT'S IRONIC THAT SOME of the very texts meant to convey the *love* of God have been abused at times in church history to reinforce the distortion of God as the cosmic equivalent of a petty, prejudiced patriarch, a big bad dad, like a cartoon image of Zeus hurling lightning bolts.

This temperamental, macho image of God turns many people off to Christianity before they ever have a chance to meet the God of creative power and tender mercies in the Bible.

There is much to say here.

While God is often referred to in the Bible with the pronoun "He," or the noun "Father," this of course is not meant to convey that God is a giant male human in the sky.

As Jesus said, God is Spirit. He has no body, so he cannot have physical gender. So what does it mean that the male personal pronoun is most often used to describe God?

For one thing, it means God is *personal*.

It means God is not an *It*. God is the *loving Father*.

Is God Male?

I understand why some translators choose to use gender-inclusive language in an attempt to avoid reinforcing negative cultural stereotypes. But I have considered their position and, in this book, have instead chosen to use the male pronoun, and male images, where they are used in the original language in the Bible.

For one thing, I think it's important to use the language the Bible uses to express truth about God. I really don't think I have already learned all I can from those words. Plus, I have yet to find an elegant alternative. Saying "He/She" or "Parent" seems to me to slightly depersonalize God precisely where God means to communicate something intensely intimate.

But there's a danger here. I urge you to be careful not to read into the biblical language ideas that are not there. You can make an idol out of words just as easily as wood. I hope in this book I show the intent behind these masculine words, and counter the stereotypes believed to be taught in Scripture by religious chauvinists—and their opponents.

I think this is especially important to hear if you had a weak, absent, or cruel father.

When male language is used for God in the Bible it is not meant to reinforce any oppressive practices in the patriarchal societies of the ancient Middle East (or any society); it's meant as a *corrective*. God is the Template, the Perfection, the Father in whom all fatherhood should find its model.

Jesus made this clear in what is probably his most beloved story, the parable of the Prodigal Son. Please read it for yourself in Luke 15:11–32.

Is God Male?

Many people have pointed out that we should really call it the parable of the Prodigal *Father*. In Christ's culture, it would have been expected that a father would disown any son who insulted him and squandered half the family fortune. But Jesus explains that God is not a father like that.

God is a father who runs to meet his son, who smothers his child with kisses, who gives gifts to someone who has done nothing to deserve them, who throws parties for people just because they are alive.

Priscilla Engle wrote a song that's been healing for so many:

"HE IS STILL A FATHER"

They tell her God loves her,
she says that's great.
They tell her he's a father
then she hesitates....

Something happened long ago
She still feels the fear
If God is like a father
Does she really want him near?

But he is still the father who loves his little girls
And he would never hurt you or destroy your world
In his eyes you sparkle like a priceless shining pearl
and he is still the father who loves his little girls

His arms are strong
But they won't hurt you
His hand is there
To lead the way
...And he'll wipe your tears away

Is God Male?

That's the Heavenly Father of Christ's parables.

And I want to point out that there is also female imagery used in the Bible for God. God patiently waits for Israel to repent like a woman in labor waits for childbirth (ISAIAH 42:14); God is compassionate like a mother who will not forsake her children (ISAIAH 49:14–21); Jesus says He longs to gather Israel together like a mother hen gathers her chicks. (MATTHEW 23:37; LUKE 13:34–35)

So is God like a Father? Yes. He is *The* Father.

But God is different in many ways than any father you or I have ever known. Or any mother. Remember, He is *Other*.

God is the source of everything good in that image of a father, far beyond what you can imagine, the Father you yearn for deep in your heart, the tender heavenly Father who longs to love, protect, nurture, and lavish good gifts on *you*.

IS BELIEF IN GOD HARMFUL?

ONE CONTEMPORARY CONCERN I want to address in a book about God: A new wave of books alleges that belief in God is actually *harmful*. Primarily through stories of abusive churches throughout history (of which, sadly, there are many examples), the argument is made that religion needs to be left behind as a relic of our primitive past.

But you could come up with random stories that appear to prove just about anything. What do *research and objective observation* actually demonstrate about the effects of faith?

Bottom line: Humans seem to be hard-wired for faith in God. Belief carries benefits far beyond the psychological...

- A 2006 study at the University of Pittsburgh Medical Center showed that improvements in life expectancy of those who attend weekly religious services are comparable with those who exercise regularly (now imagine if you both exercised and went to church)! [69]

- An article in *The Washington Times* cites various studies showing that regular church attenders have lower rates of divorce and welfare dependency, stronger immune systems, and a raft of other health benefits. [70]

- A 2011 study published in the journal *Rehabilitation Psychology* found that if traumatic brain injury victims feel close to a higher power, it can help them rehabilitate.[71]

- A Centers for Disease Control and Prevention grant allowed University of South Carolina researcher Jane Teas to interview 135 people who believed God had a role in healing them. The study was published last year and resulted in a book titled *Faith Heals: Stories of God's Love*.

- Teas writes in the book's introduction: "Our stories give testimony to a supreme presence and power of God; but not as passive, hidden in people's souls or sitting aloof on a throne in heaven. God in these stories is active, transforming the ordinary wounds of sickness and adversity to well-being and joy." [72]

One real value of studies like this is that they *refute the arguments of people who view religion as a scourge on society.*

Faith is not harmful. Instead, it seems to benefit both individuals and society.

And even atheists are noticing. In 2008, the *Sunday Times* of London printed a column by the well-known atheist Matthew Parris, who grew up in Africa but now lives in London. Headline: *"As An Atheist, I Truly Believe Africa Needs God."*

He writes:

> It confounds my ideological beliefs, stubbornly refuses to fit my world view, and has embarrassed my growing belief that there is no God. Now a confirmed

atheist, I've become convinced of the enormous contribution that Christian evangelism makes in Africa...

Education and training alone will not do. In Africa, Christianity changes people's hearts. It brings a spiritual transformation. The rebirth is real. The change is good. Far from having cowed or confined its converts, their faith appears to have liberated and relaxed them.

Christianity, with its teaching of a direct, personal, two-way link between the individual and God, insubordinate to any other human being... liberates. [73]

Put it all together and a pattern seems to emerge: Humans are wired for worship. We simply run better on faith. I really believe you and I are made for a relationship with such a God, as much as we are made for food, water, and air.

H.G. Wells was never particularly religious, but after he had studied the history of the human race, he came to an interesting conclusion:

Religion is the first thing and the last thing, and until a man has found God and been found by God, he begins at no beginning, he works to no end. He may have his friendships, his partial loyalties, his scraps of honor. But all these things fall into place and life falls into place only with God. [74]

Belief in God is not only *not harmful*—it has profound benefits. If that's true, then it's extremely healthy and productive and wise to spend time thinking about who God is.

MUSIC PLAYLIST

NOTE: If the song title is not followed by an artist name in parentheses, then it's a hymn, available from all sorts of different artists.

GOD IS HOLY AND SELF-REVELATORY

Holy, Holy, Holy
Holy Is The Lord Chris Tomlin
How Great Is Our God Chris Tomlin
Immortal, Invisible
Indescribable Chris Tomlin
Made To Worship Chris Tomlin
Revelation Song Phillips, Craig, Dean

GOD IS MAJESTIC AND OMNIPOTENT

Everlasting God Lincoln Brewster
God of Wonders (multiple artists)
How Great Thou Art
Indescribable Chris Tomlin
Praise to the Lord, the Almighty Fernando Ortega & others
Light Up The Sky The Afters
Sing to the Lord (God of Creation) Passion
This Is My Father's World
You're Beautiful Phil Wickham

GOD IS OMNISCIENT AND OMNIPRESENT

By Your Side Tenth Avenue North
Mystery Phil Wickham
You Never Let Go Jeremy Camp
Hold Me Together Royal Tailor

GOD IS SOVEREIGN

A Mighty Fortress is our God
Blessed Be Your Name Matt Redman
God Is Able Hillsong
Our God Chris Tomlin
O Worship The King

267

Music Playlist

GOD IS LOVE

The Love of God

Beautiful One Jeremy Camp

Came To My Rescue Hillsong

Hosanna Hillsong

Jesus Messiah Chris Tomlin

I Stand Amazed (How Marvelous) Chris Tomlin

Mighty to Save Hillsong

No Greater Love Matt Maher

Stronger Hillsong

GOD IS IMMUTABLE AND FAITHFUL

Be Still, My Soul

Great Is Thy Faithfulness

Enough Chris Tomlin

Faithful Chris Tomlin

Forever Reign Hillsong

O God, Our Help in Ages Past

Unchanging Chris Tomlin

GOD IS WORTHY OF WORSHIP

All Hail the Power of Jesus' Name

Awesome God

Beautiful One Jeremy Camp

Cannons Phil Wickham

Crown Him with Many Crowns

Gloria Matt Redman

Higher Gungor

How Can I Keep From Singing? Chris Tomlin

O For a Thousand Tongues

Who Am I? Casting Crowns

LITERARY RESOURCES

I've enjoyed devouring piles of books and sermons on this subject while writing this study. Many of the books I found helpful are listed here.

But! I'm afraid that I've read and internalized so much that some thoughts I now believe are my own first came from some other, wiser thinker. So I want to apologize if I have neglected to list any resources that inspired my own reflections!

Mark Buchanan, *Your God Is Too Safe*

Stephen Charnock, *The Existence and Attributes of God*

Margaret Feinberg, *Hungry for God & The Organic God*

Bill Hybels, *The God You're Looking For*

Chip Ingram, *God: As He Longs for You To See Him*

Max Lucado, *It's Not About Me*

Donald McCullough, *The Trivialization of God*

Steven R. Mosley, *God: A Biography*

Warren and Ruth Myers, *Experiencing the Attributes of God (Our discussion questions were inspired by the way this book approaches a study of God)*

John Ortberg, *God Is Closer Than You Think*

J. I. Packer, *Knowing God*

J. B. Phillips, *Your God Is Too Small*

Jarrett Stevens, *The Deity Formerly Known As God*

Lee Strobel, *God's Outrageous Claims*

A.W. Tozer, *The Attributes of God, volumes 1 and 2, The Pursuit of God, & The Knowledge of the Holy*

Ann Voskamp, *One Thousand Gifts*

MEMORY VERSES

Consider copying these verses onto 3×5 cards and keeping them in a pocket or purse throughout the study.

WEEK 1: GOD IS HOLY

Holy, holy, holy is the LORD *Almighty; the whole earth is full of his glory.* ISAIAH 6:3B

WEEK 2: GOD IS OMNIPOTENT

How many are your works, LORD*! In wisdom you made them all; the earth is full of your creatures.* PSALM 104:24

WEEK 3: GOD IS OMNIPRESENT

God is our refuge and strength, an ever-present help in trouble. PSALM 46:1

WEEK 4: GOD IS LOVE

We know how much God loves us, and we have put our trust in his love. God is love, and all who live in love live in God, and God lives in them. 1 JOHN 4:16 (NLT)

WEEK 5: GOD IS OMNISCIENT

O LORD*, you have examined my heart and know everything about me. You know when I sit down or stand up. You know my thoughts even when I'm far away.* PSALM 139:1–2 (NLT)

WEEK 6: GOD IS SOVEREIGN

And we know that in all things God works for the good of those who love him, who have been called according to his purpose. ROMANS 8:28

WEEK 7: GOD IS IMMUTABLE

Every good and perfect gift is from above, coming down from the Father of the heavenly lights, who does not change like shifting shadows. JAMES 1:17

SMALL GROUP LESSONS

LEADER'S NOTE

This study guide material is meant to be your servant, not your master. So please don't feel like you have to answer every question; the point is to develop spiritually, not to check off every question as if this were a test. We recommend that group leaders review these questions before beginning in order to select those that you think will be most effective for your group. Just be sure to allow adequate time to pray—and to discuss the group assignment—at the end of each meeting.

PARTICIPANT'S NOTE

We encourage you to look over these questions before your group meets so that you'll be prepared for group discussion. You may even want to jot down some notes about how you might answer these questions. You'll also be sharing answers from the questions after each day's reading. However, please do not feel limited to sharing only what you have written, and please do not feel disqualified to share if you have not written down responses.

SMALL GROUP LESSON 1
BEYOND IMAGINATION

CONNECT

Briefly introduce yourself to the others and share how you became part of this group.

Choose one of the following questions to answer: As we embark on this journey to focus on the wonders of God, what do you hope to get out of this study? How do you hope to personally change? Why do you need this study in your life?

WATCH THE DVD

AVAILABLE AT WWW.TLC.ORG/GODIS OR ON DVD

What is your response to the DVD segment?

In what way have you tried to "make God fit" in your life and mind?

ENGAGE

Open your Bibles and have someone read Psalm 42.

What does God reveal about Himself in this passage?

What is the connection between knowing more about God and effectively putting your hope in Him?

BOOK INTERACTION

Walk through the daily questions at the end of each devotion for this week. Share your answer to some questions that really hit home for you.

APPLY

In what specific area of your life do you need to place more hope in God right now?

PRAYER

Take prayer requests and spend time in prayer.

SMALL GROUP HOUSEKEEPING

Take a few minutes to talk about where and when you will meet next week, and who will be in charge of any meals or snacks.

Collect phone numbers and email addresses from your group members. The small group roster in the back of this book is a good place to keep this information. Just pass the books around and have each member fill in their contact info.

Select one volunteer from your group to be the Email Coordinator. He or she can help forward prayer requests around the group, and send out reminders each week about the next meeting.

SMALL GROUP LESSON 2
NOTICING GOD'S AWESOME POWER

LEADER'S NOTE

Please review these questions before beginning in order to select those that will be most meaningful and effective for your group.

CONNECT

Share a time when you felt powerless—and a time when you felt powerful.

WATCH THE DVD

AVAILABLE AT WWW.TLC.ORG/GODIS OR ON DVD

How does God speak to you through creation? Have you had an experience of God's glory through creation this week? What happened?

What prevents you from putting on those "polarized lenses" and turning daily life into an act of worship?

ENGAGE

Open your Bibles and have someone read Ephesians 3:14–21.

What is one of the obstacles you face when it comes to knowing and experiencing the love and power of God?

BOOK INTERACTION

Walk through the daily questions at the end of each devotion for this week.

APPLY

What is a situation in which you feel powerless right now? What step(s) will you take this week to give that to God?

Take a moment and pray Ephesians 3:14–21 silently, inserting the name of someone you know who needs to be encouraged by this truth. (I pray that, _____, being rooted and established in love...)

PRAYER

Take prayer requests, talk about answers to previous requests and spend time in prayer.

SMALL GROUP LESSON 3
SEEING GOD RIGHT HERE

LEADER'S NOTE

Please review these questions before beginning in order to select those that will be most meaningful and effective for your group.

CONNECT

How has this study been impacting your daily life so far? Have you experienced some special "God moments"? Have you changed the way you see creation around you?

As we begin to focus on the omnipresence of God, tell about a time when you wish you could have been two places at once.

WATCH THE DVD

AVAILABLE AT WWW.TLC.ORG/GODIS OR ON DVD

How can expecting to encounter God each day impact your outlook on life?

Review your day yesterday. How did you experience God's presence with you? Did you notice it at the time? What happened?

ENGAGE
Open your Bibles and have someone read Psalm 139:1–18.

These verses speak of God's presence in various places and times in life. Which of these images has the most impact *on* you right now—and why?

How does it help you to know that God is with you at all times? How does it challenge you?

In what area of your life do you sometimes feel like God is not with you? How could the truth of this passage help you?

BOOK INTERACTION
Walk through the daily questions at the end of each devotion for this week.

APPLY
Share with the group an area of your life where you would like to remember God's presence. Have them write this down and agree to pray for you this week.

PRAYER
Take prayer requests, talk about answers to previous requests and spend time in prayer.

SMALL GROUP LESSON 4
PERFECT IN POWER
AND PERFECT IN LOVE

LEADER'S NOTE

Please review these questions before beginning in order to select those that will be most meaningful and effective for your group.

CONNECT

How has this study impacted your attitude and actions this week? Any "God moments"—encounters with God's power or presence?

WATCH THE DVD

AVAILABLE AT WWW.TLC.ORG/GODIS OR ON DVD

How has what you've learned about God's love impacted your understanding of His love for you?

In what way do you struggle to accept and act on God's love for you?

ENGAGE

Open your Bibles and have someone read 1 John 4:7–19.

How does God show you love?

What is the relationship between loving and knowing God?

How can God's love motivate you to love others?

BOOK INTERACTION

Walk through the daily questions at the end of each devotion for this week.

APPLY

What steps can you take this week to let God's love flow through you to help you love others?

Group application: Choose a group "love project" and set an audacious goal! Suggestion: Give food and money to a local church food pantry or food bank, and agree as a group to give generously and sacrificially, and memorably!

PRAYER

Take prayer requests, talk about answers to previous requests and spend time in prayer.

SOMEONE KNOWS AND SOMEONE CARES

LEADER'S NOTE

Please review these questions before beginning in order to select those that will be most meaningful and effective for your group.

CONNECT

If you could have complete knowledge and expertise in one area of your life, what would that be and why?

WATCH THE DVD

AVAILABLE AT WWW.TLC.ORG/GODIS OR ON DVD

Honestly, does God's omniscience scare you, reassure you or frustrate you—and why?

Think about an area of your life where you've been saying, "God, don't look!" How will you begin to accept God's grace and help in that area this week?

ENGAGE

Open your Bibles and have someone read Matthew 6:1–6 and Hebrews 4:12–16.

What do these verses tell you about God's omniscience?

Often we see God's omniscience as scary and, like Adam and Eve, we want to hide from Him. How does knowing that

God is both omniscient and gracious help us run toward Him instead of away?

BOOK INTERACTION

Walk through the daily questions at the end of each devotion for this week.

APPLY

Since God is omniscient, in what area of your life do you need to surrender to His wisdom instead of your own?

Talk about your group "love project". Have you agreed on a project and have you set audacious personal and group goals for that project?

PRAYER

Take prayer requests, talk about answers to previous requests and spend time in prayer.

SMALL GROUP LESSON 6
THE ULTIMATE CURE FOR ANXIETY

LEADER'S NOTE

Please review these questions before beginning in order to select those that will be most meaningful and effective for your group.

CONNECT

Briefly share a time in your life when, for better or for worse, you felt out of control.

WATCH THE DVD

AVAILABLE AT WWW.TLC.ORG/GODIS OR ON DVD

In what area(s) of your life do you need to re-affirm that God is in control?

How could accepting and resting in the fact that God is in control impact your attitude and "hope quotient" in that situation?

ENGAGE

Open your Bibles and have someone read Isaiah 55:8–9 and Romans 11:33–36.

What do these passage teach you about God's sovereignty?

In what ways do you find it easy to acknowledge God's sovereignty, in what ways do you find it difficult?

BOOK INTERACTION

Walk through the daily questions at the end of each devotion for this week.

APPLY

In what way are you trying to control God instead of allowing Him to control you (or someone you love)? What step can you take this week to surrender control to Him?

How has your group "love project" gone? What have you learned and experienced through this?

PRAYER

Take prayer requests, talk about answers to previous requests and spend time in prayer.

ROCK-SOLID RELIABLE

LEADER'S NOTE

Please review these questions before beginning in order to select those that will be most meaningful and effective for your group.

CONNECT

God Is… How would you finish that sentence now, that perhaps you would not have when you began this study?

What are other ways your view of God has changed because of this study?

WATCH THE DVD

AVAILABLE AT WWW.TLC.ORG/GODIS OR ON DVD

ENGAGE

Open your Bibles and have someone read Psalm 145:9–13 and James 1:17–18.

What characteristics of God stand out to you in these verses?

How does knowing God does not change give you hope and courage right now?

BOOK INTERACTION

Walk through the daily questions at the end of each devotion for this week.

APPLY

What attribute of God that we studied in the last 50 days made the biggest impression on you? How did it impact you?

PRAYER

Take prayer requests, talk about answers to previous requests and spend time in prayer.

SMALL GROUP HOUSEKEEPING

Consider organizing a fun get-together as a celebration for the end of this study. Have a meal together and share how you have grown.

Is your group planning to continue following this study? When will you next meet? What will you be studying?

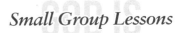

Small Group Lessons

SMALL GROUP ROSTER

NAME	EMAIL	PHONE

ENDNOTES

[1] Paul Little, *Know What You Believe*, (Downers Grove, IL: InterVarsity Press, 1968) 34.

[2] Joseph Pearce, *Tolkien: Man and Myth, a Literary Life*, (London: HarperCollins Publishers, 1998), 212.

[3] Ron Highfield, *Great Is the Lord: Theology for the Praise of God*, (Grand Rapids, MI: Wm. B. Eerdmans Publishing Co., 2008), 18.

[4] Chris Tiegreen, *At His Feet: Daily Readings to Deepen Your Walk with Jesus*, (Carol Stream, IL: Tyndale House Publishers, 2003), 189.

[5] Douglas Coupland, *Life After God*, (New York: Simon & Schuster, 1994), 352.

[6] From Bill Moyers, *A World of Ideas, Part II*, found at: www.sermoncentral.com. Stable URL: http://www.sermoncentral.com/illustrations/sermon-illustration-stories-60888.asp

[7] Linda Morris and Karl Zender, *Persuasive Writing*, (Fort Worth: Harcourt College Publishing, 1981), 135.

[8] H.G. Wells, *The Soul of a Bishop*, (New York: The Macmillan Publishing Company, 1917), 128.

[9] Margaret Feinberg, *The Organic God*, (Grand Rapids, MI: Zondervan, 2007), 48.

[10] Max Lucado, *It's Not About Me: Rescue From the Life We Thought Would Make Us Happy*, (Nashville, TN: Thomas Nelson, Inc.), 39.

[11] Garrison Keillor, *Life Among The Lutherans*, (Minneapolis, MN: Augsburg Fortress Publishers, 2010), 167ff.

[12] J. B. Phillips, *Your God Is Too Small*, (New York: Touchstone, 1997), 7.

[13] Ana-Maria Rizzuto, *The Birth of the Living God*, (Chicago and London: University of Chicago Press, 1979) 8.

[14] Stuart Hample and Eric Marshall, *Children's Letters to God*, (Stuart Hample and Eric Marshall, 1991).

[15] Lucado, 34.

[16] Lucado, 35.

[17] Anne Lamott paraphrased in Kim Peckham, *Stop Laughing: I'm Trying to Make a Point*, (Hagerstown, MD: Autumn House, 2008), 66.

[18] John Ortberg, Sermon: *The Daniel Project (Part 4)* delivered at Menlo Park Presbyterian Church, November 22, 2009. Stable URL: http://mppc.org/series/daniel-project/john-ortberg/daniel-project-part-4

[19] C.S. Lewis, *The Lion, the Witch, and the Wardrobe*, (London: HarperCollins Publishers, 2005), 80.

[20] Mark Buchanan, *Your God is Too Safe*, (Sisters, OR: Multnomah Publishers, 2001), 31.

[21] Stephen Hawking, *The Grand Design*, (New York: Random House Publishing, 2010), 162.

[22] Stephen Hawking, *"Why God Did Not Create the Universe"*, *Wall Street Journal*, September 3, 2010.

[23] Paul Davies, *"Taking Science on Faith,"* *New York Times*, November 24, 2007.

[24] Michael Denton as quoted in Jerry Bridges, *The Joy of Fearing God*, (Colorado Springs, CO: Waterbrook Press, 1997), 81.

[25] Quoted in Patsy Clairmont, Marilyn Meberg and Luci Swindoll, *The Women of Faith Daily Devotional*, (Grand Rapids, MI: Zondervan, 2002), 122.

[26] Buchanan, 149.

[27] Quoted in Sy Safransky,ed., *Sunbeams: A Book of Quotations*, (Berkeley, CA: North Atlantic Books, 1993), 63.

[28] Quoted in Skip Heitzig, *The Daily God Book: A Birdseye View of the Bible in a Year*, (Carol Stream, IL: Tyndale House Publishers, 2010), 28.

[29] Donald Spoto, *The Dark Side of Genius: The Life of Alfred Hitchcock*, (Boston: Little, Brown, 1983), 552.

[30] Greg Laurie, *Why Believe: Exploring the Honest Questions of Skeptics*, (Carol Stream, IL: Tyndale House Publishers, 2002), 19.

[31] Dorothy McInnis Scura, *Conversations with Tom Wolfe*, (Jackson, MS: University Press of Mississippi, 1990), 46.

[32] Mother Teresa of Calcutta and Dorothy S. Hunt, *Love, A Fruit Always in Season: Daily Meditations from the Words of Mother Teresa*, (San Francisco: Ignatius Press, 1987), 226.

[33] A. Fleming Seay, *Project Massive: The Social and Psychological Impact of Online Gaming* (Pittsburgh, PA: Carnegie Mellon University, May 2006), 53.

[34] Quoted in Emma S. Etuk, *Friends: What Would I Do Without Them*, (District Heights, MD: Emida International Publishers, 1999), 220.

[35] Brother Lawrence, *The Practice of the Presence of God*, (New Kensington, PA: Whitaker House, 1982), 12.

[36] A.W. Tozer, *The Pursuit of God*, (Harrisburg, PA: Christian Publications, Inc., 1948) 26.

[37] David Seamands, *Healing for Damaged Emotions Workbook*, (Colorado Springs, CO: David C. Cook, 1992), 190.

[38] Robert P. Fitton, *1927*, (Bloomington, IN: Xlibris, Corp.).

[39] Josh McDowell, *Evidence for the Resurrection*, (Ventura, CA: Gospel Light, 2009), 33.

[40] Quoted in F.W. Boreham, *A Casket Of Cameos*, (London: Epworth Press, 1926), 32–43.

[41] J. Carl Laney, *"God's Self-Revelation in Exodus 34:6–8,"* *Bibliotheca Sacra* 158 (January–March 2001): 36–51.

[42] Adapted from a story told by Stephen Moseley in his excellent book *God: A Biography*.

[43] Quoted in Robert L. Deffinbaugh, *Let Me See Thy Glory: A Study of the Attributes of God* (Dallas, TX: Biblical Studies Press, 2002), 73.

[44] Paddy Chayefsky, *Gideon*, (New York: Carnegie Productions, Inc, 1961, 1962), 36.

[45] Arthur Miller, *Timebends*, (New York: Penguin Books, 1987), 482.

[46] Richard Selzer, *Mortal Lessons: Notes on the Art of Surgery* (Orlando, FL: Harcourt Inc., 1996), 45.

[47] These and other enlightening stats found in John Cook and Karen Jeng, *Child Food Insecurity: The Economic Impact on our Nation*, Stable URL: www.feedingamerica.org/SiteFiles/child-economy-study.pdf

[48] Stuart Hample and Eric Marshall, *Children's Letters to God* and *Children's Letters to God: The New Edition*.

[49] Linda Falter, *"A Beautiful Anger," Christianity Today*, April 27, 2011.

[50] Ibid.

[51] Denise Gellene, *"Sleeping pill use grows as economy keeps people up at night," Los Angeles Times*, March 30, 2009.

[52] Quoted in Craig Brian Larson, *750 Engaging Illustrations for Preachers, Teachers, and Writers*, (Grand Rapids, MI: Baker Books, 2007), 524.

[53] Rick Warren, Stable URL: http://www.facebook.com/pastorrickwarren/posts/205807590902

[54] Billy Graham, *Just As I Am*, (San Francisco: HarperCollins, 1997), 226ff

[55] René Schlaepfer, *Thrill Ride*, (Aptos, CA: Twin Lakes Church, Inc., 2008).

[56] Lee Strobel, *What Would Jesus Say*, (Grand Rapids, MI: Zondervan, 1994), 165.

[57] Ibid.

[58] Craig Groeschel, *The Christian Atheist: Believing In God But Living as If He Doesn't Exist*, (Grand Rapids, MI: Zondervan, 2010), 13ff.

[59] Feinberg, 20ff.

[60] Stuart Hample and Eric Marshall, *Children's Letters to God and Children's Letters to God: The New Edition*.

[61] This idea is developed further in Jerry Bridges, *Growing Your Faith: How to Mature in Christ*, ch. 3.

[62] Mark Twain, *The Adventures of Tom Sawyer*, (Toronto: Belford Bros., 1876), 52.

[63] Ben Witherington, *Laying it on the Line: A Reflection on Lay Ministry*, June 4, 2011. Stable URL: http://www.patheos.com/community/bibleandculture/2011/06/04/laying-it-on-the-line-a-reflection-on-lay-ministry/

[64] Quoted in Timothy Radcliffe, *Why Go To Church? The Drama of the Eucharist*, (New York: Continuum, 2009), 58.

[65] Auguste Émile Louis Marie Molinier, ed., *The Thoughts of Blaise Pascal*, (London: George Bell and Sons, 1905), 2.

[66] C.S. Lewis, *Reflections on the Psalms* (London: C.S. Lewis Pte Ltd., 1958), 98.

[69] Daniel E. Hall, *"Religious Attendance: More Cost-Effective Than Lipitor?" Journal of the American Board of Family Medicine* (2006) 19:103–109.

[70] Jonathan Imbody, *"Health Benefits of Faith and Church"*, The *Washington Times*, April 30, 2006.

[71] Cassandra Spratling, *"Science Points to Higher Power in Health"*, *Loveland Reporter-Herald*, August 11, 2011.

[72] Ibid.

[73] Matthew Parris, *"As An Atheist, I Truly Believe Africa Needs God,"* *The Times of London*, December 27, 2008.

[74] H.G. Wells, *Mr. Britling Sees It Through*, (New York, NY: The MacMillan Company, 1916), 442.

THANKS

…to the whole community at Twin Lakes Church. I was out of the pulpit for various weekends while I worked on this, and you were always encouraging, patient, and positive!

…to my wife Laurie for her helpful suggestions and encouragement

…to Valerie Webb for overall project timeline and editing

…to Kelly Welty and his crew for the amazing small group videos

…to Kevin Deutsch for the beautiful book layout

…to Adam Nigh and Bill Butterworth for their many invaluable edits and improvements

…to Jim Josselyn for help on the small group lessons

…to June Ettinger, Ella Johnson and Caitlin Volk for proofreading

…and to the many other awesome friends and co-workers who helped with suggestions, edits, encouragement, endorsements, and more

…and to the God who Is, who, I pray, will use this book to lead us closer to Himself

Twin Lakes Church is located at 2701 Cabrillo College Drive, Aptos, California, USA.

Get small group video discussion starters, weekly GOD IS sermons, and more online at www.tlc.org/GodIs

Watch the Twin Lakes Church weekly sermons at www.tlc.org or podcast at http://feeds.tlc.org/TLCSermonVideo